To Ian
     With my
        and love.

                    John

John Tomlinson

HONEST MONEY
A Challenge to Banking

John Tomlinson

HONEST MONEY
A Challenge to Banking

Helix

First published in 1993 by Helix Editions Ltd. in the United Kingdom,
under licence from Helix Verlag GmbH, Munich, Germany

Helix Editions Ltd., Centrepoint, Chapel Square, Deddington,
Oxfordshire OX15 0SG, United Kingdom
Helix Verlag GmbH, Windeckstrasse 82, D-81375 Munich, Germany

This book was designed in Germany by Helix Verlag GmbH
and produced in England by Helix Editions Ltd.

House editor/designer: Norbert Netzer
Setting and page make-up: Typostudio & Layoutsatz
Manfred Stickel KG, Munich, Germany
Filmset in ITC Garamond; titles and headings in Benguiat
Jacket design by Alan Forster, United Kingdom
Printed and bound by Biddles Limited, Guildford, Surrey, U.K.

British Library Cataloguing-in-Publication Data

A catalogue record for this book is available
from the British Library.

ISBN 1-898271-38-0

CONTENTS

PREFACE

In this book, I wish to examine in detail one of the basic presuppositions upon which most of us have based our lives. It is one of the corner stones of Western economic thought. From Ricardo to Marx, Keynes to Mises, Hayek and Friedman to Galbraith, none of the economic thinkers who are respected today have questioned the validity of the money-lending function of the banking system. It is a "given". We are led to believe that the purpose of the banking system is to lend money, that governments and industry need bank lending to expand and create growth. These ideas should be challenged and so, too, should the foundations upon which they are built.

Bankers, like most of us, have simply found themselves within an economic and financial system which includes the practice of money-lending. Within that system they have set out to do the best job they can. Most have behaved responsibly. Yet few, if any, have examined the validity of the very function which each has so effectively performed.

Responsible bankers are not the only people busily engaged in a critical reappraisal of both the world banking system and the Western monetary system. The two systems are under threat. The former due to the current saturation of the borrowing market and the potential for massive debt default. The latter due to the potential for hyper-inflation. These threats draw the critical scrutiny of all who are responsible for them and dependent on them. In this sense the most humble saver, the ordinary working man or woman, the head of a giant corporation, and the head of a government, each share a common cause: finding and correcting whatever faults may lie within these two systems so that the application of valid remedies can strengthen them and make them more secure.

It simply cannot be right that the solution to current economic difficulty is to lower interest rates. Interest rates are lowered to entice people into debt. Nor can it be right for economists to agree that the money supply is not growing fast enough. The money supply grows by creating new debts. The inference of these two statements is that not enough people are in debt or that those who are in debt are not deep enough in debt. It is absurd to suggest that these are the means to create healthier economies.

I will expose the mechanics of the money-lending activities of the banking system: how they began as a fraud; how the dishonest money produced by this fraud-based mechanism steals purchasing power from prudent savers and those on fixed incomes and transfers it to borrowers; how this fraudulent practice was legitimised and became the principal mechanism by which our money is debased; and how inflation, business and economic cycles and other apparently unrelated market phenomena flow directly from this debasing mechanism.

I will explain why attempts to control inflation have failed and why, based on current thinking, they will continue to fail.

New thinking is essential. New thinking must be based on clearer understanding. This book is my contribution to the process of clarification.

The solutions I offer are based on what I see as being possible to achieve. They are not constrained by the 'probabilities' by which much current thinking and practice would limit us. It is possible to change the existing monetary and banking system so that it no longer debases the paper money upon which we have all become so dependent. Prices can be stabilised. The business and economic cycles to which we have become accustomed are not necessary. The mass unemployment of recessions and depressions can be avoided. Sustainable economic growth can be achieved. A continuing flow of investment into sound new enterprise is within our capability. Prudence and saving can once more be honoured and rewarded rather than penalised. All of these are possible. They can and will occur within an honest monetary and banking system. That must be our goal.

I intend through this book to contribute a perspective which is not yet widely seen, to raise serious questions about the banking and monetary systems, and to offer answers to at least a few of those questions. I have tried to avoid jargon and use the simplest of English in the interest of clarity and communication.

Steeple Barton, Oxfordshire,
Octobre 1993   *John Tomlinson*

SECTION ONE
Dishonest Money

Inflation Is Not New

A young lad was walking down the streets of Baltimore in 1937. In his pocket he had 750 dollars in cash. He was on the way to the Ford agents to buy himself a new car. As he walked along the road, he passed a bank. In its window was a poster which urged people to purchase U.S. Government Savings Bonds. He stopped.

Then, remembering his grandfather's oft spoken advice to "be prudent and save your money", he entered the bank to make enquiries. He was told that his 750 dollars would buy him a Savings Bond which would be worth 1,000 dollars in ten years' time. He decided he didn't really need a car at the moment and bought the bond instead.

Ten years later, already in possession of a good car, he decided to renew the bond for a further ten years. Then, in 1957, in need of a new car, he cashed the bond. It produced 1,450 dollars, almost twice as much as he had invested. He was pleased, and headed for the Ford showrooms. To his shock, he discovered that his 1,450 dollars would only buy half a Ford.

I was told this story more than 30 years ago, while training for the New York Stock Exchange. The lecturer was emphasising the dangers of inflation. None of us in that lecture room had had any real experience of the effects of inflation. Most of us, however, could imagine the feelings of the shocked man in the story. He had lost half a Ford, and had not had use of that money for twenty years. He would have felt robbed. Angry. And full of distrust. Who would he have blamed? Not money: money was beyond suspicion. But he would have found someone to blame for his loss.

Money which continually loses value is dishonest. It acts as a thief. It steals from those who save, from those on fixed income, and from those who enter long-term contracts. Our present society is heavily dependent on money. We rely on it as a medium of exchange: we price other commodities in terms of it. We rely on it as a store of value: any surplus money saved we expect to retain a constant value. We rely on it as a unit of measurement of exchange value: to provide a standard for interchange between commodities and goods and services both domestically and internationally. Society needs to trust money, or the whole basis of our present monetary system collapses. To trust money we need an accurate, trustworthy and constant unit of money. Yet in an era of inflation, money is continuously losing value.

To understand how inflation causes chaos, let us look at another system of measurement with which we are all familiar: time. What would happen if the unit of measurement of time continually diminished in size?

Suppose that the United Kingdom used Big Ben as the standard for time. What would happen if Big Ben suddenly developed a mechanical fault which reduces the size of each minute by one second?

Following the development of this fault, two people, each using their own, accurate, timepiece might make an arrangement to meet for lunch at twelve noon in front of a specific restaurant in three weeks' time. Both might verify their timepieces against Big Ben at some time during the ensuing three weeks. But they are unlikely to do so at the same instant. Unless they did, they would not meet. Their only other chance of meeting is if neither of them verified his watch.

Even if both did, the chances are that the restaurateur would have verified his watch at a different time, and the restaurant might not be serving lunch. By Big Ben, it would be 8.40 p.m. Our duo might manage dinner together, not lunch, and they would have to fit into the next day all the things they had intended to do after lunch.

Worse than that, each day would be getting shorter. More and more "missed" accomplishments would need to be fitted into shorter and shorter days. The rate of change of schedules and of reappraisal and rearrangement of priorities would be continually accelerating. And each and every individual, whether or not he used a faultless chronometer, would be "out of sync" with Big Ben and with each other.

Imagine the chaos. At the restaurant, for instance, suppliers, waiters, cooks and customers would each be guided by his own watch, whose degree of synchronisation would depend on how recently each had been verified against Big Ben. Cooks might have prepared food when customers did not want it. Waiters might not have arrived to serve it. Suppliers might arrive when the restaurant was closed, or the staff far too busy to receive their goods. Good luck and good fortune with respect to the timing of the comparison against official, Big Ben, time would be more important than good planning and efficient arrangement of priorities.

Planning would become suspect. Change would be the order of the day. The rate of change would accelerate. Survival would depend upon one's ability to adapt to change. "If only I had more time", would be the constant cry.

Yet man cannot create time. Time would have begun to steal from man. Time would be dishonest. Man can, however, create money. Money, like time, is one of the units of measurement which we use to determine the priority for our individual expenditure of energy. In this respect it is similar to time. Where the size of a monetary unit continually diminishes, similar effects will occur: money will steal from man.

Measuring money's dishonesty

Can we measure money's dishonesty? We can measure purchasing power in terms of other commodities. One choice against which to measure is a loaf of bread. Bread is made precisely to demand. Left on the shelf it goes stale and becomes unsellable. Historically, the one pound loaf is the most common size. Measuring other commodities against a one pound loaf of bread can give us a measure of money's dishonesty.

Consider for example, the price of oil in the years leading up to the major price increase in 1973. The price of oil had already increased substantially. In 1956, after a prolonged shut-down of its oil fields, Iran agreed with British Petroleum a price of 512.5 pennies per barrel of oil.

This would have purchased 100.8 pounds of British bread in the same year.

By 1968, the price of oil had risen to 623.4 pennies per barrel of oil; 59.6 pounds of bread. By October 1st 1973, immediately prior to the substantial increase, the price was 1315.9 pennies per barrel of oil – an enormous increase in nominal units of money since 1956. But that amount would still not buy the originally agreed 100.8 pounds of bread: it purchased only 73.2 pounds.

Value per barrel of oil

Date	Pennies	Pounds of bread
1956	512.5	100.8
1968	623.4	59.6
1/10/1973	1315.9	73.2

In terms of bread, the Iranians had been losing out for over 16 years. They had, during the course of almost two decades, lost over 25 per cent of their purchasing power. Yet, when they tried to claw back some of that loss, they suffered all the opprobrium associated with insisting upon massive increases in the price of oil.

And there we face the essential conflict about which this book is written. Money is a thief: it no longer has a constant value. No one in his right mind trusts a thief. Yet we need to trust money.

Repair Big Ben, and the chaos created by the continuing diminution of the size of the unit of time evaporates. The standard unit of time becomes a constant, and all actions can once again be synchronised. If we wish to have honest money, then we must identify and repair the fault in our monetary system so that each unit of money can have a constant value.

Creating Distrust

In the 1960's and early 1970's, a portion of the more affluent British middle class found retirement to Portugal an attractive proposition. Sumptuous villas cost around £15,000; living and maintenance costs, including a daily maid, gardener and swimming pool maintenance, were around £2,000 per annum. So on a pension of £4,000 per annum, the yearly outgoings could be comfortably met. With the gentler climate and lifestyle of Portugal, couples in their sixties were anticipating twenty years of warmth and comfort.

By 1978, many elderly couples could be found struggling with the problems of maintaining their large homes and extended gardens themselves. They often had to clean the swimming pool themselves. The mental and physical stress was not easy for them as they became older and more frail.

Living and maintenance costs had risen to £6,000 per annum. Pensions provide only a fixed income, and disillusioned pensioners faced financial hardship, if not penury. Their careful planning had gone seriously awry. Many blamed their advisers for bad financial advice, only to be told that no one could have anticipated the oil-price hike of October 16th, 1973, and the massive inflation which followed.

This is simply not true. The Member of the New York Stock Exchange who told us about the man who went to buy a Ford, warned us about the perils of inflation ten years before the oil-price hike. He was worried about the chaos that would follow the breaking of the link between the American dollar and gold. He predicted serious inflationary consequences. It is unlikely that he was the only one to see this danger. But most did not. Unfortunately, few professional advisors are prone to admit their mistakes. There is a human need to find a scapegoat: OPEC's (Organization of Petroleum Exporting Countries) actions were a natural choice.

The idea that inflation is merely a response to the increase in the price of oil is false. We have already seen how one individual, after saving the price of a brand new Ford for twenty years, was unable to purchase more than half over a new Ford in 1957. He experienced serious inflationary effects sixteen years before 1973. Those who study the history of Germany in the early twenties will confirm that inflation is not a new phenomenon – and so should any student of financial history. Yet many have vented their anger at OPEC for having brought us inflation.

When OPEC was first formed and flexed its muscle on October 16th, 1973, the West suffered a great shock. But from the perspective of the Iranians, the initial increase is not excessive. The cost of a barrel of oil was raised from 1315.9 to 2346.7 pennies. A massive increase in monetary terms – almost double. In terms of a more constant value, however, it purchased only 130.4 pounds of bread. In 1956, the Iranians had agreed to 100.8 pounds of bread per barrel. They had been short-changed by more than 25 pounds of bread per barrel over a period of 17 years.

Value per barrel of oil

Date	Pennies	Pounds of bread
1956	512.5	100.8
1968	623.4	59.6
1/10/1973	1315.9	73.2
16/10/1973	2346.7	130.4

British Petroleum acted in good faith throughout. They agreed to 512.5 pennies in 1956 and increased that by 20 per cent by 1968. They increased it a further 100 per cent by October 1st, 1973. I have seen no evidence that British Petroleum intended to mislead the Iranians in order to gain excessively for themselves. Yet Iran suffered losses. These losses eventually led them to question the integrity and sincerity of their Western trading partners.

Following OPEC'S increases many others raised the price of their product or service. Some because their costs increased, others because the opportunity was there. Everywhere the man in the street felt the crippling effects of inflation. Many demanded higher wages. They blamed OPEC or the Government or some other cause. They did not examine the mechanics of the monetary and banking system. In the long run, both the West and Iran are losers from this situation. Instead of building a better world together, they have been brought into conflict with one another. Dishonest money is the culprit.

Inflation is a problem of the Western monetary and banking system. It indicates the existence of a major fault somewhere. We need to take a critical look at the basic mechanics of the system, and find out where that fault lies. We begin by defining exactly what we mean by "inflation".

Prices increase for one of two reasons. Either the value of the product being produced increases, or the value of the commodity in terms of which the price is stated decreases. In the former case the price of a specific product will increase as a result of supply, demand, design or any other market influence which affects the product itself. Changes in these factors can also cause the value of the product to fall. Such price movements are the result of normal market activity.

Inflation, on the other hand, is a general increase in prices. All prices go up. In terms of money the value of things will have increased. The corollary is that the value of money will have gone down. Money will have lost value. Inflation can thus be seen as the loss of value by money and as purely a monetary phenomenon.

In the modern paper monetary system there is no direct connection between the production of a new unit of money and the amount of products or commodities upon which it can validly claim. Any increase in the supply of units of money will mean a decrease in the exchange value of each previously existing unit. More units will be required in exchanges to equal a given previous level of exchange value. Or, more simply, prices will go up.

21

Wrong tools

Interest rates are often used as the principal tool to control the money supply. Interest is the amount of money charged by the lender for use of his money. The payment of interest transfers existing units of money from one person or business to another. A tranfer does not create any new units of money and is not of itself inflationary.

Any increase in the amount of interest payable will simply cause more units to be transferred from the borrower to the lender. This, of course, will increase the income and profits of the lender which, in turn, will encourage him to lend more.

As we shall discover, net new lending increases the money supply. This is the real cause of inflation. If we increase interest rates we simply provide an incentive for lenders to lend more. (Witness the most recent period of high interest rates in the United Kingdom. Throughout the period of the highest rates letter boxes were stuffed with enticements from banks and other money lenders to borrow, borrow, borrow.) In the short term this is counter-productive. In the longer term it is deadly.

Increased interest rates will add to a borrower's expenses and thus decrease the amount he will have available to spend. The same process will apply to his customers who will order less, and therefore the borrower's income will be reduced. His profits will be squeezed from both ends. From the wider perspective, the production of goods and services – the wealth of the community – will be reduced and the vitality of the market-place will be sapped. Hard-working and industrious producers will find their efforts thwarted by factors beyond their control.

Increases in interest rates sap the life force of the economic system. Increases in interest rates do not cure inflation; they destroy an economy. They are the wrong tool. Inflation can only be cured by stopping the production of new units of money. The charging of interest does not produce new units of money.

We need to take a critical look at the basic mechanics of the monetary and banking system, to see exactly where the production of new units of money occurs. Then, we must remove the cause of their production. That is the minimum required to repair the fault and provide a more accurate and reliable system.

The Mechanics
of Misrepresentation

A hundred years ago, a Mr. Goldsmith opened Anybank. His first depositor, Mr. Sure, came in to lodge a gold coin for safekeeping. Mr. Goldsmith gave him a receipt. Mr. Short then came in, to borrow a gold coin, to buy a horse from Mr. Trainer. In exchange for his horse, Mr. Trainer accepted the gold coin from Mr. Short. He took it to Anybank, and lodged it with Mr. Goldsmith, who gave him a receipt. A normal set of transactions when the gold standard existed.

The strange thing about this story, however, is that Mr. Goldsmith had issued two receipts, yet he had only one gold coin. Both receipts were available for use in the market-place. Yet only one gold coin actually existed against which Mr. Trainer and Mr. Sure could validly claim. The market-place will, therefore, have been led to believe that there was one more gold coin in existence than there was in reality. So the mechanisms of mis-representation are created.

Let me take you back to the beginning of banking, to see better how this came about. Our present system is a direct descendant from the money-lending practices of the early goldsmiths. Suppose we were back in the days when trade was in its infancy, and the gold standard was just beginning, and you had some gold you wished to store. You would have several choices.

You could keep it on your person at all times: with one gold coin this would pose no serious risk. If, on the other hand, you were a wealthy goldsmith, who had large quantities of gold to store, you might require and could, perhaps, afford to build a strong-room. But, if you were in the middle, and had too much gold to carry with you at all times, but not enough to warrant constructing your own strong-box or strong-room, you might well choose to arrange with a goldsmith to store your gold on one of the shelves in his strong-room. (In those days a shelf was known as a 'bank', hence the derivation of today's word.) The goldsmith concerned would then issue you with a receipt: a valid claim against your portion of the gold in that goldsmith's strong-room.

This, of course, is what happened historically. It was, then, a natural step for holders of goldsmiths' receipts to begin to use them in exchanges, rather than using gold itself. It avoided the risk of carrying gold to the market-place. To facilitate trade the goldsmiths – or "bankers" as they became known – began to issue standard receipts for specified amounts of gold. These receipts were issued for amounts known commonly to be used in exchanges. So, when anyone took his gold to be stored he would be given a number of small value receipts for it.

The integrity of the banker was crucial to the acceptance of these receipts: the banker had to intend to, and be able to, honour each receipt. If he had issued receipts for more gold than he possessed, he would be unable to honour all the receipts issued. Some holders of his receipts would then not be able to retrieve the gold they claimed, or all would receive less than the full value of their receipts.

No paper claim or receipt is valid without this fundamental relationship. If the gold is not there, then the face value of the paper becomes irrelevant. Similarly, if the issuer's intent is suspect, then so is the claim, and that suspicion will be reflected in the way that the market-place receives his receipts.

Invalid claims

Yet there are many factors which can cause a goldsmith's receipt to be worth less than it claims to be. One is a robbery. Robbery will result in insufficient gold to meet all claims. Genuine robbery cannot be held to be the goldsmith's fault. There are, however, four factors which can be a result of the goldsmith's deliberate actions:

1. *The goldsmith might have created receipts against which no gold had been received, and used for them personal exchanges in the market-place.*
2. *He could have used some of the gold, against which receipts had already been issued, for personal exchanges in the market-place.*
3. *He could have created receipts against which no gold had been received, and lent these receipts to someone else.*
4. *He could have lent somebody else some of the gold against which receipts had already been issued.*

Each of these actions would clearly have led to an imbalance between the amount of gold actually available to honour receipts and the amount for which receipts had been issued. In each of these cases, the action of the goldsmith would have been self-serving and deliberate. No doubt some goldsmiths tried each.

The difficulty, of course, lies in knowing when they do it. If one has no access to the goldsmith's accounts, changes in the goldsmith's personal spending patterns would be the only indication that he might be using the client's gold for personal benefit. Depositors, therefore, had to remain alert to spot any significant changes in a goldsmith's lifestyle. Should any such change cause a doubt to arise, the only way of proving the goldsmith's ability to meet his issue is for all of his receipts to be presented at the same time. If they are honoured, his good faith will be proven.

Loans, however, have always been treated as confidential matters. It is not as easy, therefore, to observe the changes in a goldsmith's behaviour when he is using other people's gold to make loans, or lending receipts created without a gold deposit behind them. Such arrangements would only be of direct concern to the borrower and the goldsmith. Provided that the goldsmith behaved in a very circumspect manner, the only immediate change in consumption patterns would be in those of the borrower. (To avoid runs on their deposits which might test their ability to meet all of the receipts which they had issued, goldsmiths and their descendants, now known as bankers, have cultivated a reputation for circumspect and prudent behaviour.) The goldsmith would, however, have both betrayed trust and directly benefitted.

Lending lies at the heart of current misrepresentation. The pattern of effects which flows from the practice of money-lending can be very insidious indeed. The practice itself warrants closer examination.

One of the most immediate effects of lending is that the market-place is led to believe – unjustifiably – that there is more gold available to serve its needs. If we look again at what happened when Mr. Short wanted to buy a horse, Mr. Trainer and Mr. Sure each held a separate receipt against the same gold coin: a misrepresentation of fact. This misrepresentation is obscured by a normal accounting practice:

Deposits: 2 gold coins	*Cash:* 1 gold coin
	Loans: 1 gold coin
2 gold coins	2 gold coins

The books would thus have appeared to balance, whereas in reality Mr. Goldsmith would have issued receipts for one more gold coin than in fact he had. This imbalance would have been clearly identified had the accounts read:

Receipts issued:	2 gold coins
Stock in hand:	1 gold coin

The nature of any collateral held by the bank is irrelevant. Whatever it is, it will not be a gold coin, or the loan would not have been necessary. Nor can it become a gold coin. At most it can be exchanged for a gold coin. But an exchange does not produce another coin. It merely changes ownership of an existing coin.

So, it is clear that a fault exists in the money-lending function of the banking system. The very mechanics of the lending process produces misrepresentation: it is dishonest. Yet it has become an accepted practice. It has been legitimised.

Invalid Claims
Made Legitimate

A man in New Jersey once tried to corner the soybean oil market using a practice not dissimilar to that employed in the normal course of banking. He bought and paid for a storage tank of soybean oil. He then asked his bankers to test it for quantity and quality. He borrowed against it and bought a futures contract for the delivery of an equal amount of oil to him at some future date. He then shifted the oil to another tank and filled the first tank with water so that it would continue to appear full. He was not concerned about his borrowings, they had been covered by the futures contract.

He then had his bankers test the new tank for quality and quantity and borrowed against the new tank. He bought a further futures contract. He kept repeating the process in the hope of gaining control of the market and driving up its price to his advantage.

In each case, he had removed the real oil, and had effectively replaced it with a legal promise to deliver an equal amount of oil at some stage in the future. This is what the banking system does with our deposits. They are removed. Loan agreements are held in their stead.

Loan agreements are agreements to deliver a specific amount of money to the lender at some future date.

The soybean oil man was eventually exposed. He was tried and convicted. He went to jail for fraud. Yet bankers, who in essence do the same thing with money, continue to function as legitimate businessmen – and, in fact, they are. Their misrepresentation has been legitimised. The legitimisation occurred so long ago that most, if not all, current bankers and customers have no knowledge of it. Today, bankers are seen as the pillars of the community. No reputable economist or financial expert of whom I am aware has questioned the validity of the money-lending mechanism of the banking system. To each it is a "given".

One of the most odious effects of this misrepresentation occurs when bankers voice their objections to wage rises, arguing that such rises are inflationary. Such comments are an insult to working people. Wage earners request a wage increase to claw back the purchasing power which has been removed from their pay packets. For reasons they do not fully understand, their wages can no longer adequately support their standard of living. Demands for higher pay lead to conflict and industrial dispute. Once again we can see how dishonest money divides decent people and sets man against man.

Then we hear financiers and bankers weigh in with arguments about the workers' greed. Yet we can now see that it is not workers' greed. It is the actions of bankers themselves that are causing the losses. The injustice of their comments is appalling.

Inverted logic

As we saw with the gold coin in the previous chapter, the system produced by superimposing the mechanism of money-lending onto the system for storing and distributing money is dishonest. It ought not to have the support of the legal system. Giving legal respectability to misrepresentation turns logic on its head. The widespread use and acceptance of institutionalised money-lending leads us to believe it is a sound practice. But it is based upon misrepresentation. It is dishonest. It certainly ought not to have the support of the legal system.

Nevertheless, it does have the support of the legal system, and the amount of the misrepresentation continues to grow. The amount can be measured. In a given banking system, it will equal the amount of loans outstanding on the books of all branches of all the banks in that particular system, less the paid-up capital of those banks. Each time the banking system as a whole produces a net increase in loans, the amount of misrepresentation will increase, and the real exchange value of each previously existing unit of money will decrease proportionately.

This decrease should become immediately apparent in the market-place – but it doesn't. Under the gold standard, for instance, prices remained stable during periods when misrepresentation was continually occurring. Hidden from public view, a gap was opening between the amount of gold available to honour claims and the amount of those claims. With each new misrepresentation the gap widened. Holders of claims were unaware of it. They believed that the claims which they held could be exchanged at any time for the amount of gold stated. So long as this view held, each claim was treated as if it were the amount of gold stated.

Confidence then became the key to successful banking. It was irrelevant that a bank could not meet all its issued claims if presented for payment at the same time. What mattered was that individual claims could be met when presented. Systems were put in place to assure depositors that their deposits were safe. The presence of these systems allowed lenders to increase their misrepresentation with impunity. Nevertheless, with the increased misrepresentation, prices remained stable.

Gold had a minimum exchange value: it was in demand as the principal medium of exchange and store of value for future exchanges; it was rare; it was hard to find; it required a considerable amount of expenditure of human energy for both its discovery and its production. People would not produce it for less than the effort to produce it was worth. If demand fell and its value in exchanges fell, less would be produced. As less was produced, less would be available to service the needs of the market-place, and its exchange value would begin to increase. These factors helped to provide a minimum level below which even massive misrepresentation could not push the exchange value of gold.

As a result, there was also a minimum exchange value below which claims on gold could not be pushed unless and until holders recognised that each claim could not be exchanged for the amount of gold stated on its face. Only then would the exchange value of paper claims collapse.

This prospect faced the Western monetary and banking system in the 1930's. Had the invalid claims then been declared illegitimate, the exchange value of gold would have risen as the market recognised that there was not nearly as large a supply as had been represented. As the exchange value of gold, or money as it was then, increased less of it would have been needed in exchanges for the same previous value of goods and services. Prices would have fallen. The holders of gold and valid claims would have found their purchasing power increased. The existing amount of gold would then have been able to support an increased volume of exchanges. This was not allowed to happen. Instead, the invalid claims were legitimised, and gold was removed as a form of money.

The problems faced by the monetary authorities and banking systems in the late 1920's and 1930's were a direct result of the practice of money-lending. In the United Kingdom, for instance, up to that time, a pound was the name given to a note which had a legal claim upon one quarter of an ounce of gold. Pound notes were issued both by private banks and the Bank of England. Each accepted pound notes as deposits as if they were gold itself. Each loaned both. The acceptance of pound notes as deposits, the issuance of receipts against them, and their eventual use for loans, merely served to compound the rate of misrepresentation. The mechanics of money-lending were misrepresenting both the amount of gold in the market-place and the amount of valid claims which were issued against gold.

It took a long time before a sufficient number of individuals began to suspect that they might not be able to exchange their claims for the exact amount of gold stated. During that long period, the exchange rate of both gold and claims remained very stable at, or near, the minimum level below which gold could not be pushed. When sufficient individuals did suspect the truth of the matter, they acted with natural self-interest. The suspicious preferred not to hold notes for future exchanges: they asked for gold. The British banking system had to face the truth: it held insufficient gold to honour all the claims issued. In Great Britain, monetary collapse became imminent.

The situation was similar in North America. But it was exacerbated by the acceptance of shares on the stock market as collateral for loans. Through the provision of up to 90 per cent of the purchase price of shares in the form of loans, "bidding power" was provided which drove the share market higher and higher. At each higher level, lenders remained willing to advance 90 per cent. The value of shares soon became unsupportable. Yet "bidding power" continued to drive them higher. In due course even the most optimistic investor began to suspect that share prices had far exceeded their actual value, and would no longer invest. The market collapsed. The inflated value of collateral disappeared. Individuals and institutional borrowers were unable to sell their shares to cover loans. Lenders found much of their collateral valueless. Lending stock brokers and their supporting banks began to fall like tenpins.

So, by the early 1930's, monetary collapse in Great Britain and the United States of America was imminent. The monetary authorities of both countries ought to have recognised misrepresentation as the cause of the impending collapse. They ought to have exposed it and thereby helped the system to heal. Instead, they reasoned that if individuals had been willing to accept paper claims at a given value on one day, they ought to be able to accept them at a similar value the following day. Confidence in the exchange value of the invalid claims had to be created. Both governments therefore chose to legitimise the claims. They made them the only legal medium of exchange. They cancelled the convertibility of these claims to gold by other than governments. They banned the use of gold itself as a medium of exchange.

Thus the prudent and the careful, who had chosen to hold gold rather than paper, paid the penalty and the careless and the fraudulent were let off the hook. Dishonesty was rewarded and integrity penalised.

Nevertheless, the validation of paper money might have solved the governments' monetary problems had action been taken to stop the continuing production of invalid receipts. But nothing was done to stop the banking practice of money-lending.

Therefore the issuance of invalid receipts continued. Now, however, it was worse: the deposit looked just like the paper receipt. Both were simply statements about pounds or dollars. It is and it remains difficult to differentiate between them. Today, in the absence of a clear understanding of how the mechanism actually works, the money supply appears to grow organically. Some would even say mysteriously. Yet there is nothing mysterious about it. By allowing the superimposition of the mechanism of money-lending onto the system for storing and distributing money we have both legitimised and institutionalised misrepresentation. Thereby we have allowed the emergence of a monetary and banking system which continues to debase the currency by its own natural action.

Paper Money

If we return to Mr. Goldsmith and his new bank, and substitute a hundred dollars in paper money for the gold coin, the reason why there is no reality behind the current Western paper money system will unfold, and we shall discover why, unless the system is altered, it will collapse.

The same misrepresentation, two receipts against one deposit, will occur as it did when gold was the standard.

Accounting balance

Deposits:	$200/–	Cash:	$100/–
		Loans:	$100/–
	$200/–		$200/–

Actual position

Receipts issued: $200/–   *Stock in hand:* $100/–

Yet it will not be as easy to see. Under the paper monetary system we are easily confused. The deposit looks just like the receipt. Each is usually merely a piece of paper with the number of units of money written on it. The logic of our former example, however, does also apply with paper money: although the bank's books will balance, the money supply will actually have doubled.

We are equally easily confused when trying to determine the value of current paper money. There is no real physically measurable substance behind a unit of paper money. Nor, when a loan is made, is there any real physically measurable substance or value behind any of the newly created units of money. Nor is there any real substance behind units which are deposited. They are not guaranteed to be exchangeable for any fixed amount of anything.

Their value comes from their being the only legal and valid medium of exchange. They are effectively a claim on everything and anything that is offered for sale in the market-place. The great difficulty is that both the amount of money and the volume and mix of the goods and services against which they can claim is continually changing. There is, therefore, little opportunity to measure accurately one against the other.

If the supply of units of money were fixed, when the demand for them increased, so too would their value; and as the demand for them decreased, their value would also decrease. There would be a minimum demand for units of money. It would represent the minimum volume of exchanges required for the population to survive. Thus, each unit of paper money would have a minimum exchange value.

Each would also have a maximum exchange value. It would represent the level of exchange value at which savers are motivated to withdraw their money from savings and use it to take advantage of its greater purchasing power. A withdrawal will then increase the volume of money used in exchanges, leading to a decrease in its exchange value.

Thus, it is possible to see how a fixed supply of paper money can lead to a range of exchange values between this minimum and maximum. In due course, the exchange value of a unit of money would begin to fluctuate more and more narrowly within this range, eventually leading to stability.

Unfortunately the money supply is not fixed. New units of money are virtually produced according to demand. Bankers create new units of money every time they create net new loans. They are in business exactly for this purpose. Their normal activity produces a continuing expansion of the money supply.

Governments are meant to control the money-creating activities of banks. Current controls, however, are not effective.

Legal Reserves

A system within which each bank must hold a specified portion of its deposits in investments known as Legal Reserves has been one of the principle mechanisms by which governments have tried to control the money supply. Legal Reserves are promissory notes issued by borrowers deemed least likely to default. They are therefore the most saleable or convertible into cash in the event of an emergency.

Under this system, a bank is theoretically limited to creating new units of money in an amount equal to that of its excess Legal Reserves. If, for instance, a bank had deposits of £50,000 and the reserve requirements were 20 per cent, it would be required to hold a minimum of £10,000 in recognised Legal Reserve instruments. Suppose the bank actually held £15,000 in such investments. It would have another £5,000 which it would be permitted to advance as loans to its customers, thereby creating new demand deposits.

When we look at the banking system as a whole, we immediately expose a major weakness. The system can actually create a much larger amount than the amount of excess reserves.

Suppose, for instance, that all of the excess reserves in the system were lodged in one bank, Barclays perhaps, and that each of the other banks was willing to receive new deposits and to issue new loans to the limit of its reserves. If Barclays had the £5,000 excess referred to above, and it created new units by lending them to me, and I then spent them on one purchase at Harrods, and Harrods deposited them at the Midland, then the Midland would have a new deposit of £5,000. The Midland would then be required to invest £1,000 or 20 per cent in Legal Reserves. It would then have £4,000 in excess reserves and could lend £4,000 to one of its clients. Its client could spend it similarly, and Lloyds might then receive £4,000, invest £800 in Legal Reserves, and lend £3,200 to one of its clients. This process could continue until approximately £25,000 had been created.

Thus while an individual bank is limited to the amount of its excess reserves, the system as a whole can produce new units in multiples of the total excess reserves within it.

Nor is this limitation absolute. If we look closely at Legal Reserves, they are themselves loans. For instance, many types of government securities, including Treasury Notes, are considered Legal Reserves, and, in some cases, so are bank-endorsed bills. Treasury Notes are receipts issued by the government for money loaned to it. The government uses the borrowed money to meet it obligations. Bank-endorsed bills are also loans and are used by the borrower to meet his obligations. In both cases the money is immediately back in circulation. It will be redeposited and then it will be available to be loaned again. Reserve instruments are not a protection against misrepresentation. They are actually themselves part of the very misrepresentation they profess to be controlling.

The only limitation imposed by the use of a Legal Reserve system is the borrowing requirements of the issuers of reserve instruments. Where their appetite is insatiable there is no limitation at all.

The production of money by Central Banks

Central banks produce new units of money via several mechanisms. The most obvious, of course, is the minting of new notes and coins. In most countries it is the Central Bank which is responsible for the mint. New notes and coins are produced either to replace old and worn or damaged ones, or to maintain sufficient cash in the system to service the needs of the daily transactions in the market-place. The need for cash varies from market-place to market-place. For instance, some companies still meet their payrolls using cash in small brown envelopes. Others use cheques. Some shops and businesses will accept credit cards or cheques. Others prefer cash. Each market will vary.

Nevertheless, in general, between 6 and 8 per cent of the total money supply needs to be in cash to keep the market-place functioning effectively. The rest can remain as entries on the books of banks, representing the deposits held in clients accounts. As the money-lending function of the banking system then expands the money supply, Central Banks are required to mint more and more cash just to keep this ratio.

Central Banks also put money into the market-place by what they call their "open market" activities. In these activities they buy and sell their government's debt instruments. If, for instance, a Central Bank buys government bonds or treasury certificates on the "open market", it is not providing cash to the government. It is providing cash to the former holder of the bond or certificate who will, presumably, then either spend it or invest it. Buying, thus, is intended to create more economic activity in the market-place.

Selling the certificates and bonds held, on the other hand, takes money from investors and, provided the Central Bank does not use that money for its own or government purposes, provided that the money simply remains unused within the Central Bank, the selling activity will reduce the amount of money available for investment and spending, thereby reducing the economic activity in the market-place.

From the perspective of the money supply itself, when the Central Bank has to create new units of money to purchase bonds or certificates, the money supply will expand. Otherwise its activities will simply shift the location of existing units of money from one place to another, enticing them into savings (removing them from the market-place by a time factor), or causing them to be withdrawn from savings and spent or invested.

Foreign exchange transactions can also result in the production of new units of money by Central Banks. To see how this happens, suppose we were back in the days, when Central Banks could claim on each others' gold. Following the agreement between international Central Banks at Bretton Woods in the early 1930's individuals were no longer able to claim gold with their paper money or use gold as a medium of exchange, but governments could. Under the Bretton Woods Agreement each currency had a fixed exchange rate with the dollar and the dollar was guaranteed to be exchangable for 1/35th of an ounce of gold; or $35 per ounce.

To see how this works, suppose that General Motors in America wanted to buy Land Rover in England, before 1971. General Motors would want to use dollars, the English owners of Land Rover would want to hold pounds. The English sellers, if they accepted dollars, would exchange them for pounds at their bank. If the bank had customers who wanted dollars, it would then exchange the dollars for pounds. If the bank had no customers wanting dollars, it would look to the foreign exchange markets to exchange them for pounds. Failing that, it could exchange them for pounds at the Bank of England.

If the Bank of England had no pounds available to offer the commercial bank for the dollars, it would create them. The Bank of England would then take the dollars to New York to exchange them for gold. As a result it would receive an additional amount of gold into its reserves. So there would be no mis-representation as a result of this transaction. In fact, the real money supply (the amount of gold itself) would have increased, decreasing the gap bctwccn the amount of gold required to satisfy all claims and the amount of gold actually held.

The position in America would be quite different. Once the dollars were returned to New York, the number of dollars in the American market-place would have returned to its previous level, but the amount of gold against which the dollars had been issued would have decreased by the amount given to the Bank of England in exchange for the returned dollars. So, in America, the gap between the amount of gold required to settle all claims and that actually available would have increased. Had General Motors borrowed the money at its bank, there would have been a double dose of the increase. New dollars would have been produced against existing levels of gold, and existing levels of gold would have been reduced by the amount transferred to the Bank of England.

The increase or decrease in the size of the gap occasioned by this transaction would be unlikely to have affected the exchange value of gold in either country. In each, the level of misrepresentation would already have been sufficiently vast to have pushed the exchange rate of gold to its minimum level.

So long as the exchange rate of gold itself did not change, and so long as both dollars and pounds were considered as valid claims against gold, then the domestic exchange value of dollars and pounds in their respective markets would also be unlikely to change. Therefore, under the gold system, or the dollar/gold system (following the Bretton Woods Agreement), prices would not have increased or decreased as a result of these foreign exchange transactions. Only the size of the respective gaps would have changed.

When President Nixon closed the gold window in 1971 a new era of the paper monetary system began. The importance of this change has not yet been widely recognised. Dollars can no longer be exchanged for a fixed amount of gold. Other currencies can no longer be exchanged for a fixed number of dollars. Each country's banking system will debase its currency at a different rate. There can be no fixed relationships. The floor beneath the value of the paper money has been removed. The value of each unit can now plumb untold depths.

The same transaction under the paper money system since 1971 will produce very different results in each country. As units of paper money are no longer freely exchangeable for gold by the issuer, the dollars cannot now be returned to America to be exchanged for gold. Instead they will be held by the Bank of England as reserves.

These dollars will be held either physically outside the United States, or on deposit with the Federal Reserve Bank in New York. They will be deposits set aside as a store of value for future use by the depositor. They will no longer be part of the U.S. domestic money supply, but they will be part of the total U.S. money supply. Being removed from their domestic market-place by a geographical factor, they will no longer have a direct affect on domestic U.S. prices. But they will exist.

Their position will not be dissimilar to that of units of money removed from their domestic market-place by a time factor. A five-year deposit, for example, will play little part in the domestic market-place during its five-year term. The existence of such units of money is often effectively forgotten, only to become obvious when they mature and are redeposited as demand deposits. If inflation becomes so high that investors are unwilling to renew time deposits and will only redeposit funds as demand deposits, the money supply appears to increase dramatically. The apparent increase is false: money which had been removed by a time factor simply returns.

Similarly when units of money which have been removed from the market-place by a geographical factor return, the domestic money supply increases. But until they do return, the transaction between General Motors and the English sellers will have diminished the American money supply and reduced the amount of money available for exchanges unless, of course, the purchase was financed by a loan from General Motors' American bank.

If the purchase was financed by a loan, the new money created will have been exported. Previously existing units will not have been exported and thus the domestic money supply in the United States will remain unchanged.

In the meantime, back in England, the Bank of England will also have produced new units of money. They will have issued new pounds to exchange for the dollars received. So the British money supply will have increased.

Following Richard Nixon's decision to close the "gold window", the Bank of England is obliged to hold the dollars so acquired as reserves until market conditions change and they are needed to exchange for pounds. When they are exchanged for pounds, the pounds received in the exchange will not be destroyed. They will be used in accordance with the domestic money requirements of the Bank of England, and will remain a part of the British money supply. So the reduction in Bank of England reserves will not bring with it a commensurate reduction in the British money supply to compensate for the earlier production. The inflation produced by the foreign exchange transaction will remain in the British market-place.

When the dollars are returned to their domestic market-place, the American domestic money supply will increase and, where the transaction was financed by a loan, the inflation produced by the transaction will reach its ultimate objective: its own domestic market-place. In due course, all national currencies must return to their own domestic market-places. So the existing Eurodollar "mountain" can be seen as a continuing threat to the domestic exchange value of the dollar.

On the other hand, if market conditions were such that the dollars were required to finance a purchase in some other country, then those dollars would enter the Central Bank reserves of that other country. The money supply of the receiving country would then increase, and the inflationary effects of the transaction would be felt in yet another market-place.

Under the new paper money system, units of money removed from their domestic market-place can move from nation to nation, increasing each country's money supply en route, and leaving a continuous swell of inflation in their wake.

There are two primary dangers in this process. The one which we have already observed is the importation of inflation by the receiving nation. This can often be signalled when the reserves of a Central Bank increase. If these increases are due to the accumulation of foreign paper money, they might reflect foreign investment in

the domestic market-place. If that is the case the domestic money supply will have increased proportionately, and it follows that the domestic purchasing power
of that currency will, in due course, decrease.

The other, which is potentially more dangerous, is the
ability of international banks and the international
divisions of multinational banks to expand any nation's
money supply. Consider, for example, Eurodollars: they
are accepted as deposits and loaned with regularity by
international bankers. These deposits and loans are
unsupervised by any monetary authority. In this wider
market-place there is no international Central Bank. So
there is no lender of last resort, and no restrictions on
the expansionary money-lending activities of these
banks. The only practical limitation upon the productive
capacity of these lending institutions are the willingness
of borrowers to borrow, the credit worthiness of borrowers, and the prudence of international bankers.

Nor does the Exchange Rate Mechanism (ERM) stop
inflation. It indexes a basket of individual currencies.
Each individual currency will be being debased by its
own banking system. Each will have no floor: have no
level of depreciation beyond which it cannot go. The
rate and extent to which each will be debased must,
therefore, be different. The most that can be said for the
ERM is that it is meant to synchronise the rate of
debasement. It cannot stop it.

Imprudent behaviour

If history is an accurate guide to the future, we can con-
fidently expect to see the number of claims, receipts or

units of money in the world expand to a point of imprudence. From an historic perspective, first individual banks expanded their receipts and claims to the point of imprudence. Bank failures were experienced and the term *bankruptcy* was coined. Central Banks were then established as lenders of last resort to bail out individual banks which had reached their point of imprudence. The effect was, by giving them a safety net, to license all commercial banks to expand their operations to their individual points of imprudence. Central Banks then allowed their national money supply to be expanded in multiples, until the international banking and monetary system as a whole reached its point of imprudence. This brought the collapse of the gold standard system.

It follows logically that the international banking community will now expand the world's paper money supply to its point of imprudence. Thus we must each ask ourselves some serious questions:

Will the entire system then collapse, destroying the savings and liquid assets of everyone, including our own?

Will the system's survival instinct produce yet another palliative which allows some parts of the banking system to survive and continue their current imprudent and destructive practises, while the remainder fails?

Will our savings and liquid assets be in the part that survives or the part that fails?

Would we not be wiser to take action now to correct the system and thus avoid the risk?

Economic and Business Cycles

On an individual level, it is not difficult to see the financial hardship and emotional suffering caused by dishonest money. Our Baltimore investor could not buy his Ford; disillusioned pensioners in Portugal could no longer afford even a curtailed life-style abroad. Grandparents, investing realistically for a new grandchild's school fees, have found ten years on that they can only make a meagre contribution.

The destruction is evident, too, in the history of many individuals and businesses who found it impossible to survive the misguided cure most often advocated by economic experts and – unfortunately – also most often applied by governments: high interest rates.

As a cure, high interest rates are similar to the ancient medical practice of leeching. They, too, drain the life force from the system. The small proportion for whom leeching actually worked offer a greater testimony to the strength of the human body and spirit and to nature's continuing struggle for survival than to the practice itself. Nevertheless, at least leeching had no direct effect beyond the individual to whom it was applied. High interest rates, on the other hand, have a much wider swath of devastation.

The most recent extended period of high interest rates in the United Kingdom has left a mass of families dispossessed of their homes, an enormous number of individuals and businesses bankrupted and a significant portion of the population unemployed. The combination of these direct effects has brought economic and social devastation to many communities and regions of the country. Worse, it has destroyed the hope of large numbers of working people, the middle classes and, most devastating of all, school-leavers. None of this was necessary. The policy was wrong. Increasing interest rates is not a cure for inflation. It is, however, the habit of those who are preoccupied with measuring and controlling economic and business cycles. We must encourage them to look again at the causes of these cycles.

The creation of money by the commercial banking sector is one of the principal causes of economic and business cycles. These are a direct effect of the money-lending function of the banking system. Its role becomes more apparent when we consider the role of money as a store of exchange value.

Each identical unit of money must contain an exactly equal amount of exchange value. When new units are created without any substance behind them, the value needed to fill them must come from the value already stored by the previously existing units.

If, for instance, you lived in a small community and it had its own money, and the total existing money supply were 1,000 units, and 100 new units were minted by your local government, what would happen to the exchange value of the original 1,000 units? How can some be transferred to the recipients of the new 100 units?

The primary beneficiary of the production of these new units is the local government itself. It will put them into circulation by using them in exchanges. Perhaps none of those who accept them in exchanges will be aware that these units are newly minted and an addition to the previously existing money supply. Then the price which they ask in exchange for their commodities will not be affected and the government would receive in exchange products to the value of 100 of the previously existing units.

The ripple effect

The government of your community with its extra 100 units of money can purchase more goods and services than it otherwise could. Perhaps it will buy a new computer for one of its departments which it would not have bought had it not minted the new notes. The computer sales company will then have sold a computer which it would not normally have sold. So, too, would the computer manufacturer have made an extra sale. Each would, therefore, have made an extra profit – a profit which it would not otherwise have made. Therefore, each can spend more than it could have. If the computer cost 100 units, then one supplier will have received 100 units extra. If the computer cost only 1 unit, the government will have bought some other goods and services with the remaining 99 units and a number of suppliers will each have received a portion of the 100 new units. As a consequence each will purchase supplies from their suppliers in excess of the amount they would otherwise have purchased and each succeeding exchange on the outward ripple would occur at a smaller level of exchange value. So the benefits will continue to flow outward from the primary beneficiary in a ripple-like manner.

Each supplier along the ripple will be able to set aside as profit or savings a number of units of money which he could not have done if the government had not minted and exchanged those extra notes. The newly set aside units will allow their owners to satisfy some of their unsatisfied needs or wants. Thus, new demand will be created. The new demand will lead to either increased production or increased prices. (It has often led to a mixture of the two.)

To the extent that the increase in demand brings an increase in prices, those who have not benefitted by being part of the ripple but who purchase products whose prices have increased, will find that they have fewer remaining units of money following the purchase. They would then have to forego the purchase of some products which they would have purchased otherwise. They will have lost some of their purchasing power and their only available compensatory action is to increase the price of the products or services which they produce.

The net result in your community – all other factors being equal – will be a level of production similar to that which existed prior to the minting of the new units of money, a 10 per cent increase in the amount of money in the market-place, and a general rise in prices averaging somewhat less than 10 per cent, depending on the amount which the various beneficiaries were able to set aside as extra savings.

In addition, the government will have acquired and retained a sizeable portion of the products which had been available for exchanges. A great number of your neighbours would have had to forego products which they would normally have acquired. The market-place would have returned to its previous level of production and exchange; but exchanges would be occurring at a higher level of prices. These same processes and effects occur on a larger scale every time governments produce new units of money.

Where new units of money are created by the banking system, the effects, although similar to those produced when governments mint new notes and coins, are more complex. This is because three beneficiaries each receive 100 per cent of the new units created, and because the repayment of a loan can create a reverse ripple bringing in its wake decreased demand and decreased production.

The three primary beneficiaries are the creating bank, the banking system and the borrower. Each receives 100 per cent of the newly created units of money. Each benefits. The first beneficiary is the creating bank. Its benefit is the earning capacity of the units of money created. It charges the borrower interest for the loan. It remains a beneficiary as long as the loan is outstanding. That much is obvious.

It is not quite so obvious that the biggest beneficiary is the banking system as a whole. It continues to receive its benefit indefinitely. Once a loan has been repaid, the newly created units do not disappear. They are used to issue new loans or to meet withdrawals. When used to issue new loans, the issuing bank receives the benefit. When used to meet withdrawals, the benefit shifts to the banks which next receive them as deposits and can then use them to create new loans.

The banking system as a whole gains the benefit and retains it. Once new units of money have been created by the lending mechanism they remain in existence until there is a bank collapse. Only in that event, when some of the units stored within the collapsing bank disappear, will the number of units within the banking system as a whole diminish. The third beneficiary is the borrower. He also receives 100 per cent of the newly created units of money. He can, with those units, acquire a greater portion of the assets available for exchange in the market-place than he could have otherwise.

If, for instance, the borrower were a manufacturing company and it used the money to purchase a new machine which allowed it to increase its rate of production and if all the additional units produced could be sold, the assets acquired with the new money would provide a basis for the borrower to increase his volume of sales and, one hopes, to retain more of the units of money as profits. Or, on the other hand, the new machine could allow the company to produce the same number of products at less cost than previously.

In either case, the units of money generated by either the additional profits or the cost savings can be set aside to meet both interest payments and repayment of the money borrowed.

Negative ripples

If the assets acquired do not provide a basis for setting aside sufficient extra units to meet both interest and principal repayments, the borrower may then find himself in the position of having to reduce his overall level of purchases or his labour force in order to be able to provide sufficient units of money to meet both interest and principal payments.

If the assets acquired provide a production capacity in excess of market requirements, then either the manufacturer who borrowed or one or more of his competitors will be unable to sell all of the product which it produces. Thus one or more manufacturers will need to reduce its level of production and, consequently, its volume of purchases from its suppliers. Where the level of trade with one or more suppliers is reduced, each of the suppliers whose level of sales will have been reduced will similarly need to reduce its level of trade with one or more of its suppliers.

Thus, in either of the above cases, a ripple of reduced demand will have been produced. The reverse ripple will bring in its wake both lower levels of production and fewer units of money received in exchanges. Fewer individuals will then be able to set aside money for non-business-related exchanges, and the ripple will flow outward beyond the realm of those directly associated with the new unit of production.

There are exceptions, of course. New loans are continually being issued. Many of the borrowers use their newly acquired funds for projects which embrace common materials or components. Some suppliers will find that the level of new orders exceeds the level of completed orders, and for them and their suppliers there will be no ripple of reduced demand.

The construction industry, for instance, embraces a number of common materials. Manufacturers of bricks, glass and cement will find that their businesses can continue to expand even though the construction projects which they have supplied draw to a close and are completed. This is because sufficient new projects can be started to allow the rate of receipt of new orders to exceed the rate of completion of existing orders.

Limits to expansion

In the final analysis, all products of businesses and industries must be paid for, consumed or utilised by individuals. Continued expansion must therefore be a function of the number of individuals who have both the will and access to sufficient units of money to purchase the products of a given business or industry. Once existing demand is being satisfied by existing productive capacity, continued expansion of productive capacity becomes a function of increasing demand. So long as the numbers of individuals who want its products expand at the same rate as the productive capacity of any business or industry, then that business or industry can continue to expand. When numbers cease to expand the expansion of that industry must also cease.

There are other practical limitations to the expansion of productive activity. Without access to units of money in excess of those necessary for survival, a businessman would not be able to construct new premises, acquire new plant and machinery; nor could an individual purchase a new house, car, refrigerator or television. Responsible lenders will set criteria defining the acceptability of borrowers. Responsible borrowers will only borrow if they are confident of their ability to repay.

Once a borrower has borrowed his maximum, he must withdraw from the market-place until he has repaid sufficient to qualify again as a borrower. This can take some time. In the case of a business, new construction or completion of productive capacity must first be completed, and then the business must sell sufficient of its products for it to set aside enough units of money to both survive and repay the loan.

At the same time, the money which was borrowed would have been returned as deposits to the banking system by those who received it in exchanges. The bulk of the money would therefore be available almost immediately to potential borrowers. So, the rate at which money-lenders can satisfy borrowing capacity is in excess of the rate at which individuals or businesses can repay their loans and return to the market-place as borrowers.

In time, the numbers of acceptable borrowers who are willing to borrow must diminish as the borrowing market becomes saturated. At this point, those borrowers who are acceptable to the lenders will either have borrowed to their capacity and will be busy earning money to meet interest payments and principal repay-ments or they will be unwilling to borrow.

Therefore, the level of borrowing to expand production capacity will diminish. The sales of those who supply the goods and services used to expand that productive capacity must also diminish. It follows that the amount of those goods and services produced and the number of individuals required for their production will also be reduced.

With unemployment climbing and sales declining, fewer individuals or businesses will be capable of setting aside units of money for exchanges which are not essential in terms of simple survival, meeting interest costs and capital repayments or are production related, and even fewer products and services will be required.

Some businesses will then be unable to set aside sufficient to meet all of their essential requirements (payroll, suppliers, interest, or loan repayments), and corporate bankruptcies will ensue. More individuals will lose their jobs and the market demand for products will shrink still further. Thus a major economic contraction begins.

A fall in demand or an excessive productive capacity in some specific business or industry is not sufficient to cause a major contraction. Even during a period of booming economic expansion, markets change and some products and services go out of favour or are replaced by technological advancement.

No, a major economic contraction stems from an excess of lending by the banking system as a whole. It will reflect the saturation of the total borrowing market for a particular banking system and will therefore encompass the entire market-place which that banking system services. Demand in general will fall because few will be in the position to borrow and spend. Of course, there will be exceptions and some businesses will thrive and expand (accountants specialising in bankruptcy, for instance), but the bulk of the ripples will reflect negative demand.

The rate at which a negative ripple can move or grow is much more rapid than that at which an expansionary ripple can move or grow. An expansionary ripple moves at the rate required to construct new productive capacity. A contraction, a negative ripple, requires no more time than is necessary to decide to cease using existing productive capacity.

So economic and business cycles are one of the results of having superimposed the mechanism of money-lending onto the system for storing and distributing money. As we have seen earlier, other effects are:

1. *Inflation.*
2. *The destruction of the role of money as a unit of measurement of exchange value.*
3. *The destruction of the role of money as a store of value for future exchanges.*
4. *The redistribution of purchasing power and thus of wealth from savers to borrowers.*
5. *The impoverishment of those on fixed income.*
6. *The rewarding of dishonest behaviour and the penalising of honest behaviour.*
7. *Social distrust and divisiveness.*

There cannot be any doubt that allowing this super-imposition to occur and to be institutionalised has been a major error. It cannot be allowed to continue. The serious question to which we must now address ourselves is: How best can we remove it?

Piecemeal Solutions

The Aswan dam, when it was planned and first constructed, was hailed as the solution to Egypt's irrigation and flooding problems. Yet viewed from hindsight, the problems that such a magnificent feat of engineering caused are mamoth. The fishing industry, which used to rely on sardines from the Nile delta for a substantial proportion of its income, saw its annual catch of 18,000 tonnes drop to little over 500 now that there was no longer a flow of alluvial silt to provide feeding grounds for the sardines. In addition the snails which carry the bilharzia-producing liver fluke no longer died in the winter months in the empty irrigation canals, so the disease spread, bringing with it widespread disability.

When the decision was made sixty-odd years ago at Bretton Woods to stop the convertability by anyone other than governments of paper money to gold, governments and financiers alike believed that the problems of the Western monetary system were solved. It was hailed as an economic achievement of enormous magnitude, perhaps as great as that later attributed to the engineering achievement of the Aswan dam.

61

With hindsight we can now see that it, too, brought with it a new league of problems: ones to which, as yet, there have been no permanent solutions. The question which we must now ask: Can any of the currently attempted solutions be developed to provide a durable correction?

The most simplistic theorists would say that the market should solve its own problems: that the banking system should be self-correcting. Others would say that there are sufficient natural constraints on money-lending to avert crisis. The reality is somewhat different.

The system does, of course, have some natural constraints; it would otherwise have collapsed by now. There are two natural limitations which have helped to contain the inflationary explosion. The first is the time lag between a deposit and a withdrawal. Bankers need to maintain sufficient money on the shelf to meet withdrawals. Although norms are established, market conditions can lead to large increases in the volume of withdrawals without apparent prior notice. Prudent bankers therefore have tended to maintain reasonably large excess reserves in order to meet these should they occur.

The second is the existing net asset value against which bankers are willing to lend. All of the assets which bankers are willing to accept as collateral have a measurable exchange value at any given point in time. Bankers are willing to lend only a portion of that exchange value against each asset. The sum total of all of those portions tends to provide a practical ceiling limitation upon the total volume of money which banks do create. Bankers themselves are unwilling to create more once these portions have been fully loaned.

Even this ceiling is not absolute. The actions of bankers themselves force a rapid elevation of it. This occurs because of the "bidding power" which lenders provide. Potential purchasers of a specific asset can obtain from their banks a commitment to provide an agreed portion of the eventual purchase price of that asset. Each potential purchaser can then gear his "bid" according to his other available money and his expectations from that asset.

For example, if you and I were each seeking to buy the same house, we would first obtain from our respective mortgage lenders the proportion of the sale price which they would provide. Suppose each agreed to provide 90 per cent. If the asking price was $100,000, we would each need about $10,000 to make a successful bid or offer. Suppose you had $10,000 in savings and offered the owners their asking price. If I had $12,000 in savings, I could offer them up to $120,000 and outbid you. If they accepted my offer, the market value of the house would have increased. "Bidding power" would have led to the increase.

Where there are a number of assets, and a number of bidders, the assets can change hands quite often. This can produce the effect of a continuing increase in the sale price of each asset. The upward spiral of increasing prices can continue to grow until it becomes obviously unsustainable: lenders will then withdraw further "bidding power" or potential bidders will withdraw from the market; or both will occur simultaneously, triggering a fall in the price of the assets. If the rate of price increase has been sufficiently disproportionate and rapid, the level of exchange value of these assets can then collapse to their former levels or less.

This is what occurred on Wall Street in the late 1920's where publicly listed shares were the assets against which "bidding power" was provided and lenders were willing to finance 90 per cent of the price. When potential purchasers of shares began to question whether the rises in share prices could be sustained and many declined to buy, prices began to fall. They had to fall only 10.1 per cent before their price was less than the amount which had been borrowed to purchase them.

Before that point was reached, however, the borrower would have been called upon to put up more money to reduce the loan to a level of 90 per cent of the new value of the shares. When borrowers could not provide the money required by these "margin calls", the shares were sold – which drove prices down even further. As a result of these forced sales in which often both the borrower and the lender lost money, share prices were driven further and further downward. The losses were on such a scale that many who had borrowed to purchase shares were forced into bankruptcy. So, too, were many of the stockbrokers which had provided the loans to the buyers and many of the banks which had provided loans to the stockbrokers.

It was this same "bidding power" which caused the price of property to rise so spectacularly and then to collapse so catastrophically in London in both the early 1970's and late 1980's. In both of these "boom and bust" cycles property, not shares, was the collateral for the loans. In the "bidding" process, each purchase was funded by new loans. Net new loans produced new units of money. The end result was a continuing increase in the supply of money in each market-place.

In the United States, following the Wall Street collapse in 1929, as a result of the inability of either failed share purchasers or failed stockbrokers to repay their loans, many banks also collapsed. Their depositors thus lost their deposits. This had the opposite effect. It reduced the money supply. Thus, much of the inflation produced in America by the "bidding" process in the 1920's did not survive.

In the latter cases, however, in London in the 1970's and the 1980's, systems were in place to protect deposits and there was no widespread bank collapse. Deposits were not lost. The money supply did not shrink and the inflation produced by the "bidding power" remained. With respect to inflation, Central Banks and depositor protection have been counter-productive.

Nor can we find much comfort in attempts to cure inflation. Economists and governments, in devising methods for curing inflation, have placed emphasis on the effects and not on the causes. As a result, the solutions which have been attempted have treated the symptoms rather than the illness.

Attempted cures

Consider, for instance, the wage and price policies which have been tried. Returning to our earlier "Big Ben" time analogy, these policies can be compared with attempts to limit one or other section of the community to but one verification per year of the watches of its members against Big Ben. The lack of synchronisation with the remaining sections of the community would produce similar effects to those in the time analogy.

The two people who agreed to meet for lunch but didn't check their watches against Big Ben would actually meet for dinner according to official time and, therefore, would have had to squeeze all the things they had planned to do after lunch into their schedule for the following day. The days would also keep getting shorter and more and more missed programmes would have to get squeezed into these shorter and shorter days. Time would continually be being lost.

Restricting the income of some will mean that those who have been restricted will continually be losing purchasing power and they will have to put off some purchases until another day as they feel the effects of this lost purchasing power. The continued application of such a policy will erode first the net disposable income and then the financial safety margins of both individuals and businesses. This can so damage an economy that any consideration of these policies as a solution to anything is unacceptable and has proven so wherever tried.

The level of prices or wages has to do with the distribution of units of money which already exist. The level of wages has to do with the distribution of the units of money received by a business or an industry. The level of prices has to do with the distribution of units of money which enter the market-place. An increase or a decrease in either level can only change the location of existing units of money. Neither can create one new unit of money.

Inflation, however, is a result of the production of new units of money. It has nothing to do with the distribution of existing ones. Solutions cannot be found in controlling the distribution of units of money. Price or wage controls, therefore, will not stop or even reduce inflation. They will, however, disadvantage the section of the community affected by the controls.

The level of government borrowing is another "red herring" which has been blamed for causing inflation. The level of borrowing, either government or private sector, has to do with the distribution of units of money available for investment. Increases or decreases in this level cannot create one single new unit of money. Changing investment distribution from the public to the private sector accomplishes nothing in the fight against inflation. The attack must be waged against the lender whose actions actually produce inflation. The attack must not be waged against the borrower.

If the lender lends what already exists, against which no previous claims are outstanding, and if it is his own and he recognises that he will be without its use until it has been repaid, then the market will not be misled and there will be no inflationary effect. It is only when the lender lends that against which prior claims have been issued, or creates new claims against exchange value for which prior claims have already been issued, that existing claims are debased and inflation rears its ugly head.

Nevertheless, in utter frustration, even indexing has been attempted. In our "time analogy" example, this can be compared to connecting every church bell in the United Kingdom to Big Ben, so that those within earshot can re-set their clocks and watches every hour on the hour as the nation's bells peal. Although this, too, appears to be a reasonable solution, its absurdity becomes apparent when one observes the relationship between "official" Big Ben time and natural time. In the second month, for instance, it will be dark at official noon and light at official midnight. In due course, two "official" days would fit into one natural day. It is a nonsense.

The time analogy is useful in that it shows us exactly how a mechanical fault can lead to an ever increasing rate of change. The time analogy also helps us to see why some of the accepted programmes have failed to cure inflation.

One of the most commonly used methods for controlling inflation is to increase interest rates. Although interest rates were dealt with earlier in this book, it is worth restating the arguments. Interest payments are also about the distribution of money that already exists. They transfer units of money from the borrower to the lender. The transfer of units of money from one to another does not create one single new unit of money.

Increases in interest rates are also counter-productive. They entice lenders to lend more. Worse, they squeeze businesses at both ends. They increase costs. This reduces the amount a business has for other expenses. So, sales decline while costs increase. This drains the economy. It leads to increased unemployment and increased personal and business bankruptcy.

Yet, increasing interest rates remains the preferred tool used throughout the Western world in the fight against inflation and reductions in interest rates remain one of the principal tools used to encourage economic activity. While lower interest rates do serve a useful purpose in that they reduce the running costs of existing borrowers, that is not the real purpose for the reductions. Interest rates are reduced in order to encourage more people and businesses to borrow and spend and, thereby, to increase the levels of both production and employment.

When looked upon dispassionately, this latter use of the interest rate tool is perverse. Lowering interest rates encourages more people and businesses into debt in the name of building a healthier economy. It claims that the economy is less healthy than it could be because either not enough people and businesses are in debt or because those that are in debt are not yet deep enough in debt. Yet it is debt that destroys individuals, businesses and, ultimately, economies. The use of interest rates as a tool for manipulation or control of economic activity ought to be immediately abandoned.

Monetarists have recognised that it is increases in the money supply which create inflation. To this extent they are correct. Their solutions, however, deal with the distribution of existing units of money. Their solutions are misguided. If we are to stop inflation we must stop the production of new units of money.

The Hourglass Is Emptying

Is Western society running out of time? Can we afford to ignore the warnings? One economic crisis seems to follow another; each downturn seems to plunge the Western world into a deeper recession. We have had the Third World debt crisis, the collapse of the U.S. savings and loan associations, two U.K. property crises, the Japanese stock market has collapsed, the international exchange value of both the dollar and the pound have fallen dramatically, the ERM is under immense strain, German re-unification is undermining the strength of the Deutschmark, and we have had three major economic downturns – culminating in the recession of the early 1990's, the worst since the depression of the 1930's. All of these have occurred since President Nixon closed the "gold window" in 1971.

There can be little doubt that the imprudence of the banking community has played a major role in each. These crises may now be signalling to us that the international banking system has already expanded the world's money supply to its point of imprudence. With no international lender of last resort, collapse of the world monetary system must be a strong possibility. Indeed, the establishment of the Bank for International Settlements as a "World Central Bank" has already been mooted. Yet the establishment of an international Central Bank can only temporarily avoid the eventual collapse of our existing paper money system. It could bail out existing central banks which have difficulties. They could in turn bail out existing commercial banks which have been imprudent. But, we've seen all of this before. That's how Central Banks came into existence in the first place.

In the early days of banking, when depositors began to worry about the security of their deposits in a particular private commercial bank and all arrived simultaneously to withdraw them, because the bank had built its business on the back of misrepresentation there was not sufficient money available to repay every depositor. Either some depositors would lose all of their deposits or all depositors would lose some of their deposits.

This, in turn, would raise questions in the minds of depositors in other private commercial banks and would often pose a threat to the survival of all banks and their deposits. It was under these circumstances, where the interests of both banker and depositor coincided, that Central Banks were born. Under pressure from both depositor and banker alike, governments established Central Banks as lenders of last resort. The newly created Central Bank could then provide funds to meet withdrawals where commercial bankers could not otherwise meet them. Thus, the existence of Central Banks ensured the continuity of both the customers' deposits and the commercial banks.

Herein lies the problem. By providing a safety net to bankers whose misrepresentation had reached its point of imprudence, Central Banks allowed the misrepresentation to continue and gave it legitimacy. What we now face is the result of allowing this behaviour to continue: imprudence on a massive scale by governments, Central Banks themselves and the commercial banking system as a whole.

The establishment of a "World Central Bank" can only prolong the agony. It will license the continued imprudence of governments, central banks, and commercial banks. Each will then be free to continue its habitual misrepresentation until a new point of imprudence is reached. Following that, there can be no higher level upon which to create a lender of last resort. There will be no further way of underpinning the world's monetary system. Eventually any system based on misrepresentation must collapse.

Individual governments are pursuing a relentless path of economic expansion, without heed to the consequences. From their perspective, it appears that the only way out of a contraction is to create an expansion: to change the negative ripples for positive ones. But the changes required to create an expansion weaken the system.

In the course of a contraction, those borrowers who can survive the decreased volume of exchanges and still set aside sufficient units of money to repay their debts will do so. Their repayments will help to strengthen the position of the surviving banks. When the banks have received sufficient units of money through repayments and new deposits, they may feel confident once again to begin to expand their lending activities. But many borrowers who have proven their worthiness by repaying their loans will have no need to borrow to expand existing productive capacity. Excess productive capacity will still exist in most industries. Thus the bankers' natural drive for expansion will be frustrated.

To continue to expand its lending business, the banking community has historically had to look beyond its list of previously acceptable borrowers. Criteria were adjusted so that the borrowing market could be expanded to embrace a larger proportion of the population. This has required a lowering of standards of credit worthiness, weakening the assets against which depositors' money has been secured. Emphasis has shifted from the financing of productive capacity to the financing of consumption. These changes in criteria have allowed the banking system to increase its overall lending. Increased lending means increased interest earned: means increased profitability: means increased inflation.

Yet it is this propensity which leads to a repetition of both business and economic cycles. As lending is expanded, the number of ripples which provide benefits will increase, and, in due course, a general expansion of the economy will once again begin. The difference between a business and an economic cycle merely relates to the extent of the market-place affected. At the root of both is the money lending activity of the banking system.

Each general expansion has been followed by a general contraction. The duration of each general contraction has been determined by the length of time required for the banking system to re-build its reserves through the receipt of debt repayments. When their reserves have become sufficiently strong for them once again to begin seriously to expand their lending activities, historically they have often had to look to a wider market of acceptable borrowers. Even here the hourglass is emptying: there is little room for expansion.

Initially the privilege of borrowing was restricted to the wealthy, to those individuals who possessed assets whose value far exceeded the amount borrowed or who possessed sufficient power to command the money with which to repay a loan. Property owners, merchants, industrialists, kings, princes and governments could borrow. Today it is not even necessary to have assets. Tomorrow's pay – unearned units of money of unknown future value – is now acceptable as collateral. Thus the borrowing market has been expanded from yesterday's rich and powerful to embrace today the most humble of society's working men and women.

Certainly in the Western industrial countries it is difficult to envisage an expansion of the borrowing market so as to embrace more individuals. But where is the market beyond the West? It is unlikely that the wage levels in non-industrial nations would allow their wage earners sufficient borrowing capacity to fuel a significant expansion of the lending activities of the Western banking system. Over the course of history, long-term contracts have kept the real prices paid to many less developed countries for raw materials at a low level. Witness the combined effects of long-term contracts and inflation on the purchasing power received per barrel of oil by the National Iranian Oil Company. It was not until the major oil producers in the world united to form a cartel that they held sufficient power to raise the price of oil and redress their losses. Few other producers of the raw materials required to fuel the manufacturing processes and standard of living of the Western industrial nations have been able to unite to form such cartels.

During this same period, wage and price levels in the industrialised countries have increased substantially. So, too, has the cost of finance and the cost of plant and equipment. The net result is that, in the West, raw materials now often represent an unrealistically small portion of the cost of production.

In addition, many of the principal producers of these natural resources, whether they are mines producing ores or large farms producing foodstuffs, are also the principal employer in their local economy. This leaves them in the position to maintain downward pressure on the level of wages that they pay to the local work force. In one province of the Dominican Republic, for instance, there is one principal bauxite mine and little else to provide employment. There is thus little competition for local employment to provide a balancing upward pressure. The same can be said of many of the mines in Africa and of much of the sugar-cane production in the Caribbean or Central America.

Wage earners of less developed countries have, therefore, not been able to command a high level of wages and earnings are substantially lower than in the industrial West. Expanding the borrowing market to include the working people of the less developed countries cannot produce a consumer-led boom of any consequence in the industrialised nations.

On the other hand, an expansion of the borrowing market in these countries can lead to economic growth in their own markets. This is what is happening in the Pacific basin. Korea, Taiwan, Singapore and Malaysia have booming economies. China is following closely. Industries in these economies will compete with the industries of the West. They have their own expanding banking systems. In time they, too, will be unable to expand further.

Very real limits to the progressive march of expanding and contracting cycles do exist. These cycles can only continue until all existing borrowers and potential borrowers have borrowed to their maximum, thereby saturating the borrowing capacity of the entire world population. After that there can be no major expansion of the borrowing market. Any expansion which could follow would have to be a result of repayment of existing debt or expansion of world population. Neither can occur at a rate sufficient to fuel a new expansionary wave.

It could also happen that, before the borrowing market becomes totally saturated, total world productive capacity might so exceed that required to satisfy world demand that no one would seriously contemplate the construction of any new productive capacity. Without the construction of new productive capacity there will also be no major expansionary wave.

Yet expansion of the money supply is required to produce the new units of money necessary to meet withdrawals and maintain customer confidence. Without continuing expansion the banking system cannot survive. Without new lending the current banking system cannot expand. Without change the future of the Western monetary and banking system looks very bleak indeed.

SECTION TWO
Honest Money

The Requirements
of Money

Major changes are obviously required if the collapse of the monetary system is to be averted. Before undertaking any change, however, it is vital that we have a clear picture of the requirements of sound money and a sound monetary system. We must know where we are heading. Honesty and accuracy must be the prerequisites.

Money serves three specific functions. It acts

1. *as a unit of measurement of exchange value;*
2. *as a medium of exchange; and*
3. *as a store of exchange value for future use.*

No commodity which continually loses value can be acceptable as a unit of measurement or as a store of exchange value for future uses. Any commodity which physically deteriorates, tomatoes for instance, will inherently lose value, and therefore will prove unacceptable.

The commodity used most successfully for money to date has been gold. By its very nature it is almost ideal. It is scarce. To produce a small amount of it requires a large expenditure of human energy. It is homogeneous and therefore can be divided into small amounts of identical size, quality and exchange value. It is inert: it does not physically deteriorate, so it does not inherently lose value. It passes the first hurdle. But there are other hurdles.

Supply and demand play a part in determining the exchange value of any commodity. Demand in the case of money must reflect the amount needed to service the numbers of and value of exchanges in the market-place. Where survival is dependent upon exchange, people will need money to buy food, drink and shelter. As a result there will be a minimum demand for money equal to the amount required to feed, house and clothe the total population.

Both the numbers and the value of exchanges will change as the size of the population and its expectations change. So increases in either the population or its expectations will produce increases in the demand for exchanges in the market-place and, consequently, increases in the demand for money.

Any commodity suitable for use as money must also meet the requirements of ordinary people for their normal use in the market-place. It must be available in quantities sufficiently small for an individual to carry enough on his person to use for expected daily exchanges. The product used as money should therefore be such that it can be divided into small equal and identical lots and that a small amount of it carries a relatively high exchange value. Thus a commodity which is scarce and homogenous would suit. Gold meets both these requirements.

Any commodity which is scarce will require a large expenditure of time or energy to locate and produce it. If the exchange value of money were to fall, those involved in its production should consider producing something else. The level of production would then decrease. It would fall until the demand sufficiently exceeded the supply, and then its exchange value would begin to rise. This rise would encourage more producers, and, as the supply increased, its exchange value would once again begin to fall. Over the course of time its level of exchange value would tend to fluctuate less and less, eventually leading to price stability. It is important to note here that the control of the supply of the commodity used as money is the willingness of people to expend their energy producing it.

Ideally, the product chosen as money would have a level of exchange value as near to constant as possible. To achieve constancy the product would have to be available in such quantities and in such conditions that each measurable unit of human energy would produce exactly the same amount of it, and each amount produced would have exactly the same level of quality. Gold does not have this quality. Nor has such a product yet been found. Therefore the ideal unit of money has not been achieved.

There is nothing magical about gold which demands that it be used as a medium of exchange. It is true that gold has more of the characteristics that best serve in a medium of exchange than any other natural commodity. Over the course of time, people have come to recognise this fact. Should it ever be legitimised again as a medium of exchange, there is every indication that people will once more use it in that capacity.

Paper money, on the other hand, is not a natural commodity. It is man-made. Man, therefore, ought to be able to control it. The weaknesses which need to be controlled are the following:

1. *Paper money can be produced too easily.*
2. *It is subject to wear, damage and destruction.*
3. *There is no relationship between the cost of its production and its exchange value: its production is limited only by self-restraint.*

We know that any increase in the supply of paper money will remove exchange value from the holders of previously existing notes, and transfer it to the recipients of newly created notes. We know that increases in the money supply under the paper money system will reduce the size of the unit of exchange value and produce all the distortions which were observed earlier.

It is clear that no production which will increase the existing supply can be permitted. Therefore, if we are to salvage the paper money system, procedures will have to be put in place which ensure that no notes can be minted except for the replacement of worn or damaged ones. In addition, the money-lending activities of the banking system will need to be brought to an immediate halt. The control procedures required will need to be very exacting and rigorously enforced.

When such procedures are firmly in place we will experience phenomena in the market-place which have been long forgotten. With any general population increases or with any increases in the level of expectation of the existing population, the level of exchanges will increase and so, accordingly, will the demand for money. Where it is not possible for the supply of money to increase, any increase in demand for it will lead to an increase in its exchange value. This means that prices will fall and the same amount of money will service an increased volume of transactions. So, we will discover that an economy can expand without requiring an expansion of its money supply.

Of course, there is a catch: as money's exchange value increases, some people will prefer to hang onto their money rather than use it in exchanges. Hoarding and dumping could then lead to artificially large swings in the level of exchange value of money, which in turn could seriously disrupt the market-place.

This is a hurdle which can easily be overcome. Increases in the exchange value of money will lead to people preferring to use something other than money in exchanges so that they can hold on to the money which is increasing in value. Buyers will offer sellers a choice of substitutes instead of money for the goods and services which they wish to purchase. Eventually exchanges will occur using substitutes acceptable to both parties. In due course some commonly acceptable substitutes will emerge. If these commonly acceptable substitutes were also made valid as legal tender or units of money, then the money supply would expand according to demand.

This time, however, the expansion of the money supply would be very different to that which we currently experience. Each money substitute would have its own previously existing level of exchange value, so it would not remove any exchange value from existing holders of paper money and the value of money would remain relatively constant.

Therefore, we can now see that it is possible to develop a programme which can maintain the existing paper money system, stabilise the level of exchange value of existing units and provide us with a total money supply which can expand naturally according to demand. This must be our goal.

A Major Re-Think

To see how best to achieve the goal we set above, we will have to consider the legal framework within which money trades and is invested. It is most likely that any country wishing to have sound money will have to change existing legislation.

For instance, in most countries, contract and tax law have created a market-place where debt investment is given advantages that equity investment is not. If we look at the decisions individual investors have to make, we can see why.

People wishing to store money for future exchanges have several choices:

1. *They can store it in a safe.*
2. *They can exchange it for some other commodity, product or property.*
3. *They can exchange it for whole or part of a business venture.*
4. *They can lend it.*

Storing money has the disadvantage of cost. Safe and secure storage facilities are not free. Whether the investor rents space, or builds his own storage facilities, costs will be incurred. If the exchange value of money does not increase, then there is nothing against which to offset these costs, and the amount stored will be reduced by the cost of the storage. To reduce storage costs, less secure facilities might be an option. But this increases the risk of loss: a loss which could be total.

The saver can exchange his money for some other commodity, product or property which might increase in value more than money will over the period. But, there is a risk. Exchange is permanent. The value of any commodity, product or property could also fall. The saver might then incur a greater loss than he would have from paying for storing units of money. Products and commodities also have to be stored during the period of saving and properties have running and maintenance costs.

A permanent exchange is also involved in an equity investment. An equity investment is an exchange of units of money for a proprietorship, a partnership, a joint venture agreement or a shareholding in a company. The exchange is permanent. The investor will no longer have money. The investor will now own a bit of something. It can be called "wealth" but it will not be money.

A successful equity investment will mean that the exchange value of the equity will increase and that its portion of the profits generated will provide its owner with an income. There are genuine clear risks associated with any equity investments. Its value can fall as well as rise. A business, for instance, may not make a profit; it might fail. In which case its investors will not receive any income: worse still, they could lose their entire investment. But the risks are born only by the investors.

Lending is also a form of investment. It is only a temporary exchange and thus avoids the risks that accompany permanent exchange. By lending, investors merely give the use of their units of money to someone on a temporary basis. The exact amount loaned must be returned on a specific date. Debt agreements and claims on collateral are enforceable under the law. Lenders can use the law and the law-enforcement agencies to help them to collect their debts. The law-enforcement agencies are required to use their time and energy, payed for by the taxpayer, to help to prevent lenders from losing either the amount of money loaned or the interest payments due on it.

If your home is repossesed, it is the servants of the courts who reposses it. If you are made bankrupt, it is the courts who make you bankrupt. So, taxpayers are required to spend their money in order for the lender not to lose his. Even when a court sends receivers into a business which has been made bankrupt, the costs of the receivers are paid for by the bankrupt business. If there is any equity remaining which might benefit the owners, it is out of these interests that the costs are first taken.

The existing legal arrangements are designed to protect lenders from losses associated with investments into which they have freely entered. The reality behind a failed loan, however, is that the lender has made an error of judgement in making the loan in the first place. His error can be seen as the same error that was made by the borrower. Both believed at the time the loan was agreed that it would be able to be met. If it cannot, both have made the same mistake. The law, however, treats one error rather differently than the other.

In fact, looking at the choices an investor has to make, an astonishing degree of legal bias is evident. Businesses do fail, for a variety of reasons: sometimes insufficient planning, sometimes insufficient capital; ineptitude, or even dishonest or dishonourable behaviour. An equity investor will have to bear the full responsibility for his own error in judgement: possibly facing total loss. The debt investor, on the other hand, has a substantial degree of protection: taxpayers place at the disposal of the lender the full support of police departments, bankruptcy courts and, in some cases, even prison services, to help the lender recover what he can of his investment.

The effect of this is to allow lenders to transfer what they can of their recovery costs to the taxpayer. Taxpayers, therefore, are required by law to waste their money in order to minimise the losses of lenders. Collective society gives to lenders a shield of protection which it denies to equity investors. Where debt finance is concerned, the risk is taken first by the borrower, second by the taxpayer and only then by the lender. Equity investors must bear the risks by themselves.

The discrimination in favour of debt investors actually goes much further. Governments, through tax laws, allow interest payments to lenders to be made from pre-tax profits, while insisting that dividend payments to equity investors can be paid only from those profits which remain after tax has been deducted. Therefore businesses must earn significantly more to give an equity investor the same return as a debt investor.

If, for instance, you loaned £100 to a business at 6 per cent interest, that business would have to earn £6 before taxes to pay your interest charges. Had you bought £100 worth of shares in the business, it would have had to pay taxes before it paid you a dividend. At a 33 per cent tax rate, the business would have had to earn £9 and pay £3 in taxes before it would have had £6 after taxes to pay you as a dividend.

As a result, investors find themselves positively encouraged to structure their investments so as to use the maximum amount of debt investment and the minimum amount of equity investment. In this manner they will pay less tax. On the other hand, by allowing this bias to continue, governments will receive less tax from the business community than they would otherwise and as a result individual taxpayers must shoulder a higher proportion of public expenses than they would otherwise.

Lenders have been granted special privileges under the law. What does the taxpayer get in return for granting these privileges? Lenders' actions debase our currencies producing inflation, they cause the business and economic cycles which lead to very high levels of unemployment and they produce the many other social and economic distortions which have been identified earlier in this work. Further, their interest charges are the fastest growing and the most significant section of the very government budgets to which ordinary taxpayers are being asked to support disproportionately.

It is time to level the playing-field. Why should taxpayers continue to spend their money in order to minimise lenders' losses? Haven't government budgets enough to do as it is? Why should lenders' income be subject to less tax than the income of other investors? Why should everyone else continue to put up with the divisive and destructive effects which follow in the wake of this fundamentally flawed money-lending mechanism?

We should insist that the law be changed so that money-lenders have to bear the full cost of their own errors in judgement, so that ordinary taxpayers will no longer be required to subsidise any portion of the recovery cost of lenders' errors in judgement and so that profits in general are all taxed on the same basis.

The statutes which protect money-lenders are the sinews which bind the money-lending function to the banking system. Without them banks could not lend with security. These laws can be changed so that all debts, like gambling debts are now, are declared unenforceable. Money-lenders would then have no more security than equity investors. They would not be able to lend depositors' funds with any degree of certain repayment.

Depositors would no longer continue to have confidence that banks which loaned money will be safe depositories for their cash or savings. Would you have confidence that your money would be safe if you put them in a bank which used them to make legally uncollectable loans? If something went wrong, how would you get your money back? Banks would have to cease their lending activities.

A money-lender would be totally dependent upon the integrity of the borrower for the return of his investment; an equity investor would have both the integrity of his associates and the ownership of his portion of any assets involved. Equity would suddenly become a more attractive option.

Existing statutes and taxation policy can be changed: where tax advantages and debt-collection support are provided for lenders, governments can alter policies and statutes can be amended or removed from the statute books. These changes will not prohibit money-lending as a form of investment. Individuals will still be free to lend money if they wished. They will simply have to bear the risks themselves.

Changing the law would simply be an open declaration that society is no longer prepared to protect money-lenders from their own errors of judgement. Taxpayers would no longer pay for the errors in judgement of money-lenders. Court, bailiff and police time could be freed for more useful purpose. It would add loan debts to the position already occupied by gambling debts. They will not be legally enforceable. Illegal methods of debt collection will not be tolerated for loan debts any more than they are for gambling debts. Lack of security would then bring about the demise of money-lending as the standard method of finance.

Credit would certainly continue. If credit worthiness is already established, credit arrangements will be likely to continue. Producers will still need to produce and sell their products. If you were running your own business, manufacturing widgets for example, and this change in the law came into existence, you would be bound to review all your customers and their credit facilities. You may well continue to issue credit to those whom you knew to be people of integrity and who paid your invoices promptly. Others will cause you to consider carefully the risk involved with issuing them further credit facilities.

You will have to decide, in each case, between the benefits of various levels of production of widgets, the size of the order and the likelihood of not being paid. No doubt you would end up with some customers of whose integrity you were fully confident and others of whose integrity you were less confident but whom you believed for one reason or another would be most likely to pay. The degree of risk would be tempered by both the need to stay a profitable business through maintaining a minimum level of production and by the amount of profits generated at various levels of production.

This need to stay in business will ensure the continuation of consumer trade and credit. But the risks involved will be taken only by the individuals and businesses offering the credit. That is not the case today. Today, banks provide the credit and, in doing so, produce the inflation which steals purchasing power from each unit of money and puts at risk savers and those on fixed income.

Those who issue credit will have recourse only to the integrity of the individuals involved, regardless of their financial strength. Without knowledge of the integrity of those with whom one is dealing, few would risk their cash or savings. Today, the personal integrity of those to whom credit is issued is often of less importance than the ability of those who issue credit to enforce the terms of their agreements under the law. Without recourse to the law there will be a growing and ongoing demand for personal integrity. Human behaviour will have to change.

The above proposed changes in the law can be approached in one of two ways:

1. *Existing debt can be allowed to continue under the current framework, so that only debts incurred after a specific date would become legally unenforceable.*
2. *All debt can be made immediately legally uncollectable.*

If the second option is chosen, the changes in the law must also simultaneously convert all existing debt to equity – except in those instances where both parties agree to continue the investment in the form of a debt.

Any changes made must provide just and equitable treatment for both existing lenders and existing borrowers. There will always be unscrupulous borrowers who, given the opportunity, will simply refuse to repay their debts. At a minimum, each existing debt investment will have to be converted to some proportion of the ownership of the venture in which it was invested.

Banks would thus receive shares in the businesses to which they had loaned money. Conversely, to the extent to which banks had insufficient cash to match deposits, each depositor would receive shares in his particular bank.

The simultaneous action of repealing the laws which protect money-lenders and converting debt to equity can benefit society in the following ways:

1. *It will stop the production of new units of money by the banking system. This can bring inflation to a complete halt, and it will stop the leakage of exchange value from existing units of money. Savings and frugality can then, once more, be encouraged.*

2. *It will convert to shares many units of money which have been removed from their domestic market-place either by a time or a geographical factor. This will preclude their re-entry into the domestic money supply and the consequent reduction in exchange value of the units already there.*

3. *It will stop the re-distribution of exchange value by the banking system. Purchasing power would no longer be removed from depositors and transferred to borrowers. Removal of this re-distributive mechanism will reduce the need for a taxation system designed to re-distribute it once again.*

4. *It will help to re-establish the merit of a venture itself as the principal factor in investment decisions. Historically, banks have only tended to lend to those with acceptable collateral. Those whose ideas and projects have merit but who have no acceptable collateral, have often found raising capital difficult. For equity investments, the investor's security rests solely in the success of the venture itself: equality of opportunity based on merit would suddenly become a reality.*

None of this will happen by wishful thinking. Legislation will be required. Following legislation, a considerable period of adjustment will ensue before stabilisation occurs. Nor will the passage to a healthier economy be an easy one. The Western economies are currently desperately ill. Palliatives have been tried and they have failed. They now need major surgery and time to heal. In our final two chapters, we therefore look at the nature of the surgery involved, the necessary steps to heal the system, and the benefits that can result.

Serious Surgery

The question must now be asked – and it is a serious and hard question: do we wish to change our current dishonest banking and monetary system for an honest one?

If we do not, then this is no more than an academic exercise. If we do, we can actually begin the process of seriously addressing the problems of inflation, debt, unemployment and growing government budget expenditure.

Of course, none of us is free to wave a magic wand and make it all happen just as we wish. But, each of us is capable of thinking the problem through, learning what needs to be done, and influencing our political electees. Have you ever noticed how, when enough people set the right example, their leaders follow?

The steps required to stop the creation of new units of money by the banking system are fairly straight forward. Legislation will have to be enacted which makes new loan agreements legally unenforcable from the date of the Act. The Act will have to deal with all existing law which offers protection to any sort of lender, depositor or creditor. It will have to remove any form of debt collection, any assistance to debt collectors and any action against debtors – including bankruptcy – from the police, the courts and all other areas of government authority, except perhaps in matters of taxation, for debts incurred, credit given or deposits made after the date of the Act.

Option 1: allowing existing debt to continue

Under this option, there will be no change for debts already in existence, credit already issued or deposits made prior to the date of the Act. They will be enforceable under the law applying at the time of the agreements into which the parties entered.

The changes required in taxation rules will require a similar approach. To put interest payments and dividend payments on a level playing field, either dividend payments will have to be allowed as a deduction before tax is calculated or interest payments will have to be made from profits after tax. With respect to existing debt, many companies are so dependent upon debt finance that they would not be able to meet interest payments from profits after tax. For them to survive, they would have to continue to pay interest from income before tax. Where existing debts are allowed to continue, therefore, the tax rules which existed immediately prior to the Act must continue to apply to debts incurred before the Act.

Following these changes, debt will no longer be an attractive option and the money-lending activities of commercial banks and the banking system as a whole will cease due to lack of security.

Existing debt will be repaid over time, as their various maturities are reached, bringing home units of money which have been removed from their domestic market-places by either a time or a geographical factor. The real domestic money supply will then become apparent and the process of accurately measuring both its domestic and its international exchange value can begin. But, this process cannot begin until all existing debt is repaid. That could be a long time indeed.

For many, these changes will not be enough. They leave the current extensive burden of debt in place. Businesses could still be made bankrupt under the law covering existing debt. Interest payments will still be required. Either could continue to add to the growing roll of the unemployed.

The cost to taxpayers of interest on government debt is gigantic. This is a cost about which many can ask valid questions. Why, when the government is the only legally authorised creator of money, do governments license others to create it and then pay interest to those whom they have licensed on the new money created? It is more normal for licensees to pay royalties or fees of some sort to whoever grants the license. Banks should be paying the governments fees. Governments should not be paying interest. Elimination of interest payments from government budgets can reduce them substantially.

Option 2: converting all debt to equity

The conversion of all existing debt to equity will resolve these additional concerns. Complete conversion is a more radical and thorough solution. It will, of course, require a more complex legislative package. The nature of the relevant legislation will obviously vary from country to country. The purpose here is merely to outline the essentials.

New legislation will be required to repeal all existing law which offers protection to any sort of lenders, depositors or creditors. It must also, except in the areas of taxation, immediately remove from the jurisdiction of the police, all courts and all other areas of government authority, any form of debt collection, any assistance to debt collectors and any action against debtors – including bankruptcy.

Simultaneously all existing debt must be converted to equity. Conversion will be an enormous task. Title to the unpaid portion of goods will need to revert to the seller or to the finance house, depending on which had issued the credit. An exception to this can only be allowed when both parties agree to retain an investment as a debt – so long as each party acted in the full knowledge that the debt will no longer be legally enforceable.

To resolve any bona-fide disputes which will naturally arise from the above two acts, a system of special Courts of Equity will need to be established, to which parties unable to agree can appeal for arbitration or determination. These courts can be self-financing, deriving their costs from fees set as a predetermined portion of the disputed equity. Fees would be paid proportionately by each contestant in a ratio determined by the court. It will be in the interest of both parties to settle before fees are imposed. Pressure would be on each to find a basis for agreement and thus to avoid these costs.

The conversion of all debt to equity will raise questions about the strength of the various claims on the actual cash held by each bank. There will not be sufficient cash in any bank to meet the claims of all its depositors. Claims will have to be honoured in some order of priority. Current or cheque account depositors who have lodged their money in the bank for safe-keeping, should have a preferential claim to those who deposited their funds in interest-bearing accounts for investment purposes. The latter would then find themselves actually having to bear the risk of investment.

Unsatisfied deposits will have to be converted to shares in the bank itself. Each bank is a borrower from its depositors. So, each deposit remaining after the allocation of cash will have a claim on a portion of the total remaining assets of the bank. By issuing shares in lieu of cash banks will become giant holding companies, owned by both the banks' original shareholders and their unsatisfied depositors, each in proportion to their particular contribution.

Individuals in debt will have to issue shares in their assets in lieu of debt. Companies in debt will have to issue shares in themselves in lieu of debt. Lenders will thus become part-owners of the assets which their loans helped to acquire. As a result, individuals or existing shareholders may no longer be able to retain full control of assets acquired through debt.

In the case of individuals, it may be that joint ownership of an asset is established with one or more of the lenders becoming entitled to exercise control over that portion of the assets reasonably agreed to represent the unpaid loan balance. If the asset was, for instance, a house, a fair rental can be determined for its use, and the borrower will be required to pay his new co-owner the appropriate portion of the rental. Or, if agreed, the house may be sold. The borrower and the lender will now each own a portion of the house. Each will be entitled to his share of the proceeds of the sale.

In the case of a company, new shares will be issued to replace debt. New shareholders will be entitled to excercise their voting rights and control may shift to the new shareholders.

Governments are amongst the biggest borrowers. Converting their debt to equity is a different matter. While governments can issue shares in their tangible assets, they cannot issue shares in themselves. They can, however, mint new notes and coins in a quantity sufficient to equal the total of any government debt remaining after the conversion of government owned tangible assets to shares.

The actual physical printing of money is seen by many as inflationary by definition. This is not necessarily the case. Some printing of new notes is not inflationary. To the extent that banks had loaned money to governments, the new money created would simply return to the banks as tangible units against which depositors could legally claim. The money supply would then not increase. Its form would merely change. Depositor claims without real substance behind them would become depositor claims with substance behind them.

Repayment of government debt to lenders other than banks by this method will simply give actual physical substance to units of money removed from the market-place by a time factor. Of course, once returned their presence will be felt. But that would have happened anyway. When the debt had matured, they would have been returned as demand deposits and their presence would then have been felt. The worst that can be claimed about minting new notes and coins to repay government debt to other than banks, is that it will bring forward the timing of inflation which was already in the pipeline and due to occur at some future date.

Sound Money

Once the production of new units of money by the banking system had ceased, and once sufficient notes and coins to repay government debt have been printed, and once forgery is adequately controlled, and once governments and Central Banks are prohibited from producing new notes and coins – even for foreign exchange transactions – except to replace damaged or worn ones, there will be no means of expanding the paper money supply. Money will then seek its own realistic level of exchange value.

The new notes and coins minted by the government will cause an increase in the money available for exchanges, so there will be one further decrease in the exchange value of money. This means one further round of inflation. After that, there will be no more debasement of the currency and thus no inflation to follow in its wake.

To what extent will this minting of new notes increase the money supply? Perhaps an exercise I did some years ago can shed some light.

In America, as of June 1985, total government debt stood at approximately $6,525 billions. The money supply, including both cash in circulation and bank deposits, stood at $3,136 billions; less than half the government debt. There, if none of the government debt were owed to banks and the newly minted notes and coins went directly into circulation, the money supply would increase about three times to $9,661 billions. The United Kingdom presents a similar picture. As of the same date, the money supply stood at £138.5 billions, while total government debt was £170.7 billions: the money supply in the United Kingdom would increase at most 2.25 times.

To the extent that the government owed money to the banks, the newly minted notes and coins used to repay the banks would be placed in the banks' vaults and would be available to be claimed by depositors. They would become part of the previously measured money supply and so the size of the increase would be less. The repayment of government debt has another important benefit. Once new coins have been minted to clear the debt, governments will no longer need to service their debts. No interest payments will be required. Their budgets can be significantly reduced. This will benefit all taxpayers.

Having by these processes established a stable, limited, money supply, it is important to remind ourselves of how the boundaries of exchange value are set. Natural human self-interest might well, at a time of concern about the value of money, discourage people from holding it. The resulting lack of demand could push the value of money below its realistic level. Many might then not want to hold money. Demand for it could fall further. But demand for exchanges cannot go below the level required for the survival of the popul-ation. Therefore the demand for the medium of exchange will also have a minum level. With a fixed money supply the minimum level of demand for money would, in due course, be discovered.

Of course, there is also a concern about how high the value of money can go. To avoid hoarding as the value of money increases, thereby reducing the amount available for exchanges and forcing the value of money even higher, substitution can be encouraged. If substitutes are legally acceptable as currency, the demand for money will be reduced by the amount of the substitutes accepted in exchanges and the upward pressure on the exchange value of money will be accordingly reduced.

Under normal conditions, as time progresses, both population and the expectations of that population will increase. This will lead to both an increase in the demand for money, and an increase in the norm around which the exchange value of a fixed money supply will fluctuate. The introduction of substitutes will help to avoid an increase in the level of this norm and thereby will help to promote price stability.

Control forgery and limit the minting of new money to the replacement of worn or damaged stock, and the total paper money supply will not be able to increase. Any increase in total bank deposits will be limited to that coming from private storage, or returning from foreign countries. These figures are accurately measurable and predictable within reasonable tolerances. By keeping a watchful eye on the total of all bank deposits, both domestic and foreign, those responsible for any currency should soon detect any leakage and its source.

The processes of re-assessment

Once this non-money-lending fixed paper money supply system is established, two processes of re-assessment will occur: the value of money will be measured and re-assessed in terms of goods and services and the value of goods and services will similarly be measured and re-assessed in terms of money. Both processes will be part of each exchange transaction. Thus, the processes of re-assessment will occur continually, every minute of the day, hour by hour, day by day, transaction by transaction.

Until the value of money begins to stabilise, there will no doubt be much more negotiation and haggling over prices in restaurants, shops and other retail outlets than there is now. Prices will not be fixed. The precise value of money will be uncertain. So, too, will the strength or weakness of the position of both buyer and seller be uncertain. In due course, however, the value of money will begin to settle and buyers and sellers will begin to recognise their respective strengths and weaknesses.

As people come to recognise that the value of money has begun to reach its bottom, some will begin to set units aside in the hope that their value might rise. Inevitably the value of money will begin to rise and prices will begin to fall. We will then be presented with a new problem: there are mechanisms in place for altering the prices of goods and services both upwards and downwards but there are no mechanisms for adjusting wages and salaries downwards when the value of money increases. This is an area which will need attention.

If your salary begins to buy more than it did, you will be delighted. The difficulty will arise if you are an employer. As prices decline, so too will the number of units of money received by the business. The exchange value received may be the same but the amount of money will be less. If the amount of money paid in wages and salaries remains fixed, employees will receive a greater portion of the wealth produced, profitability will be squeezed and the survival of the business will be threatened. In the processes of negotiation which will naturally follow, the interdependence of manager, employee and shareholder will become more obvious. Out of this recognition can grow mutual respect and co-operation.

From the perspective of those of us who might wish to put something aside for the proverbial "rainy day", we will no longer be able to avoid real decisions by using debt as a method of storage or investment. We will have either to store our money, or exchange it permanently for something else. Storage and distribution will become a more expensive option than currently.

Banks would no longer have the benefit of interest income to carry most of their operating costs. They might gain some income from brokerage fees on share exchanges and for other financial services which they might choose to offer, but these will not fully replace interest income. So, in addition to having to become more efficient, full storage and distribution charges will have to be introduced. Leaving money in a bank will become an expensive choice.

Equity investment will prove a more attractive option to most of us, whether it be in shares, a partnership, our own business or simply buying a commodity, a product or a property which we believe will increase in value. Those of us who receive dividends from our investments will also be more likely to invest it in equity investments rather than to store it. Thus, the portion of the money supply which seeks investment will be constantly being renewed and measured against the investment opportunities on offer.

There will be a continuous flow of capital seeking equity investment. Either it will go into new ventures, commodities, products or properties or it will be used to buy existing ones from previous equity investors. In the latter case, the previous equity investor who sold will then have the money and will face the same choices. The net result will be a continuous flow of new capital available for new equity investments. Sustainable economic growth is a natural result of an equity-based economic and monetary system.

Nevertheless, some will wish to store money itself for future use. They will either pay the rate for storing it in someone else's facilities or they will provide their own. This private hoarding would cause a decrease in the amount of money available to service the existing level of exchanges. Demand for money will then increase. As a result the exchange value of the money will increase and prices will fall.

The decreasing prices will produce two separate effects. The first is that it will draw units of money back from savings. Some who have stored cash will want to take advantage of the increased purchasing power gained during the period of storage. As they bring money from storage and use it in exchanges, the amount of money available for exchanges will increase. The value of money will then fall and prices will increase.

The second effect is, as we noted earlier, that it would draw money substitutes into the market-place. When the exchange value of notes and coins increases and individuals are tempted to store or hoard their money, each will need to find something else to use for exchanges. Substitution will occur. No doubt some will use gold in exchanges. Others will simply barter their own products or services. Perhaps barter will become a more common practice once again. In any event, in due course, some other products will become commonly acceptable as media of exchange. Each of these practices will allow the money supply to expand at whatever rate is required.

The net result of all of these processes will be the establishment of a norm around which the value of units of money will fluctuate. As greater experience is gained by all involved in these new market activities, a tendency to narrow the range of the fluctuations will grow. In time this will promote genuine and sustainable price stability.

New function for banks

The changes in the law which are proposed will not themselves lead to the closure of any banks or the system as a whole. There are still valid and important functions to be performed. The need to store money safely and to distribute it efficiently with minimum risk will continue. Depositors wishing to exchange their money for shares will need to be brought together with those seeking capital. The existing staff in most branches of most banks are in the best position to assist in each regard in each local market as well as to provide both information and connections through their national networks.

At the same time, through the conversion of debt to equity, banks will have themselves become large holders of shares. Much of the loans which they had previously issued will have been converted to shares whose value will need to be determined. This valuation will, in turn, help to determine the value of shares in each bank which will now be owned by many previous depositors. In each respect, existing banks are a logical place to begin to develop the new market for shares which will emerge as a result of those who suddenly find themselves with shares when they need cash and those who intend to invest rather than to store money.

The natural activity of the market-place will also begin the process of measuring the exchange value of goods and services more precisely and more accurately. The alternative to exchange is storage: those choosing to put their money to work rather than pay the cost of storage will exchange it for a share in a business venture, a property, a commodity, a product or a service. Each carries risk. So each potential investor will need critically to examine the merit of each potential investment.

The permanency of exchange requires careful judgements about present and future value. Products of poor quality with built-in obsolescence are unlikely to maintain their value in terms of either investment or consumer acceptability. Quality and durability will need to be more accurately assessed.

The arrangements which the proposed system would require to finance housing illustrate the need for critical judgement. Debt investment, or mortgages, would no longer be an option. Those wishing to purchase a home would have to seek co-owners on an agreeable shared-ownership basis. Each of the co-owners in a particular house, whether they be an individual or a company, would own an exact portion of that house. The resident owner would pay the appropriate rental to each other owner. There could, if required, also be an agreed programme between the resident owner and his co-owners by which he could purchase from them additional equity, eventually owning his own house completely.

Whatever the arrangement, the value of each co-owner's investment would depend on the value of the house. If its condition deteriorated, each investor would lose. Investors might well be very chary of many of today's construction practices. The use of green soft wood which warps and deteriorates over time may not be acceptable to the critical investor. Construction materials which have proven the test of time will be sought after. Their use will assure the investor that his investment has less risk of deteriorating and thus less risk of losing value. Similarly, owner-occupiers who have a reputation for caring for their properties will be sought after. Those who do not care for their properties and have a reputation for neglect will find it hard to raise equity-based finance.

New perspectives

Every product, every service, every commodity, every bit of land, will be viewed from this new and critical perspective. Each and every individual will also continually have to re-assess the size of the unit of measurement of exchange value from his or her own perspective. That measurement will then need to be applied to the products of his or her own energy.

Each different measurement will have an effect on another. The resulting changes will work their way through the market-place. The dynamic of change will be considerable: continual re-assessment in the light of changing conditions and priorities.

The extent of the interdependence of owner, shareholder, manager, employee, supplier and customer will be more readily apparent. Each business will be a joint venture. The individuals in its component parts will act with self-interest. Continuing co-operation at all levels of business will be vital to continued prosperity.

World-Wide Changes

Applied on a world-wide basis, the conversion of debt to equity and the printing of notes and coins to repay government debt, can also resolve the international debt problem. From the perspective of individual nations with foreign debts, it offers a practical means for liquidating their foreign debts without the domestic political and economic sacrifices now being demanded.

Meeting foreign debts

Non-government foreign debts can be met by share issue, in the same fashion as non-government domestic debts. Government foreign debt can be met in the same way as government domestic debt. New notes and coins can be printed to the value of the foreign currency owed by the government at the exchange rate prevailing immediately prior to the payment. It can then be given to foreign creditors as payment in full.

In some cases, this would lead to a substantial proportion of a nation's money supply being in foreign hands. Consider, for instance, the money supply of the following countries from my 1985 study (as of June/July 1985; presuming no banks hold government debt):

Currencies in billions (bn)

Nation	U.S.	U.K.	Brazil	Mexico	S. Africa
Currency	Dollar	Pound	Cruzeiros	Pesos	Rand
Current money supply	3,136.0	138.5	161,580.0	10,475.8	45.3
Govt. debt domestic	6,349.9	158.5	205,501.0	7,200.0	43.2
foreign	175.5	12.2	676,401.0	21,933.6	53.3
U.S. dollar equivalent			($113.3 bn)	($96.2 bn)	($22 bn)
New money supply	9,661.4	321.8	1,043,482.0	39,608.8	141.8

Had each of the above nations converted their total government debt at that time and at those rates, each would have experienced a growth in its total money supply. The United Kingdom would have experienced the least growth, the United States and South Africa would have each found its money supply to have exceeded three times its previous size, Mexico would have found its money supply almost quadrupled, and Brazil's would have increased six and a half times. But there it would end: there would be no further increase. Holders of each currency would look forward then to a stabilising influence rather than the current continued diminution of the level of exchange value.

112

Effects on domestic money supply

With the exception of the United States, the amount of money in each domestic market-place initially would have doubled. One third of the total South African money supply, half of that of Mexico and two thirds of that of Brazil would be held in foreign hands. This money would only find its way back into its domestic market-place when it was used by its foreign owners to purchase products exported from, or to travel within, its country of origin.

If Brazil, Mexico and South Africa were each to provide a framework for foreign investment that was attractive, external holders of each currency would wish to invest in those countries. The increased level of economic activity provided by these investments would bring an increase in the demand for money. The increase in demand for money would help to offset its loss of exchange value caused by the return of foreign-held units. Repayment of debt by this method would then trigger a substantial investment boom in each country.

Of this group of countries, the United States alone would immediately experience a substantial increase in domestic money supply: by a factor of three. Therefore the exchange value of the dollar could be expected to be reduced by two thirds and prices and wages could be expected to treble very quickly.

Yet the American dollar would also gain enormous strength if a world-wide programme of conversion were to be undertaken. Eurodollars do not appear in the above figures. They are dollars which have been permanently removed from the American market-place, lodged in non-American banks and in non-American debt instruments.

Through a process of lending and relending, the number of such dollars has multiplied to a sum many times the U.S. domestic money supply. The potential for these Eurodollars to return to the United States now poses a major threat to the domestic value of the U.S. dollar.

In a world-wide conversion programme, however, Eurodollars would be converted to shares or other currencies. Eurodollar loans to borrowers in the private sector would be converted to shares. Eurodollar loans to governments would be converted to the currency of the particular borrowing government. Eurodollars would disappear. The threat which now hovers over the U.S. dollar would no longer exist.

The figures above portray the maximum possible increase in the money supply of these nations. In fact, the increases could be significantly less. To the extent that nationalised industries and other government-owned assets can be converted to shares, the amount of paper money required to repay government debt will decrease. To the extent that banks have lent to government, the newly minted notes and coins would be used to repay despositors and would not, therefore, represent an increase in the money supply.

CONCLUSION

Converting debt to equity is not a panacea for all economic ills. It can, however, produce many positive benefits. These benefits will not necessarily follow automatically from conversion. Concentrated effort will be required to ensure they do. Without conversion they will not happen at all.

Not the least of these benefits will be those brought to the banking community itself. The banking and monetary system will not collapse. Nor should there ever need to be the threat of collapse again. Owners of banks will find the value of their shares underpinned as liabilities disappear from balance sheets and are replaced by assets of a specific value. Each and every depositor will be able simultaneously to withdraw his or her total deposits.

Demand for the banks' current or cheque account services will not diminish. Longer term depositors will now have to pay for storage: it will be a less attractive option than exchange, so the velocity with which money moves from bank to market-place to bank again, from one account to another, is likely to increase. There will be a continuous flow of money available for new equity investment.

The market-place in general will also receive benefits. Conversion will allow the value of money to stabilise. Savings can then retain their value. Prices need only vary according to the supply and demand of the product being priced. Measurements of exchange value made by different people at different times can be validly compared. The unit of money will once more be a valid unit of measurement of exchange value. The field of economics can become a science.

Many of the distortions which now exist in our individual frames of reference will be corrected. For instance, an investment which took an investor ten, fifteen or twenty years to recoup used to be considered sound. Now, too often the maximum period envisaged is five years; even three. This short-term view has precluded many useful businesses from being created. The re-establishment of stable money and the emphasis on security which will be required within equity investment programmes will encourage people to take a longer view. More businesses will then be considered viable and the number of new jobs can increase dramatically.

Existing savers will also be protected. The conversion to equity will eliminate the possibility of collapse for individual banks and for the system as a whole. Savings will not disappear. The nature of savings will change from just units of money to units of money and shares. The exchange value of both the shares and the money will have to be re-assessed. But they will have value. If no action is taken and the system collapses, they may end up having no value.

The changes proposed will also free many from the enslavement of debt. Both nations and individuals can regain their dignity. They will be free to make their own choices. No longer will managers have to face the choice between paying interest and disemploying some or not paying interest and disemploying all.

Nor shall we need to experience the stresses caused by current economic and business cycles. There will be a steady flow of money into investments. New investment opportunities will continually be sought as a home for both individual saving and business profits. Both will wish to avoid storage charges.

Growth will be dependent upon the continuing development of new ideas and new productive capacity. Growth will no longer be dependent upon the creation of new debt. Economic expansion will depend upon the positive flow of new savings and new profits.

Re-establishing the integrity of money will eliminate at least one of the causes of human conflict. Money will no longer secretly steal from those who save, those on fixed income and those who enter long-term contracts.

Further, it can lead to a greater premium being placed on personal integrity. The character traits of honest, honourable and forthright behaviour will be in demand. Investors' security will depend on them. Recognition of the degree of interdependence in an equity-oriented market-place can lead to more consideration of the needs of others, and, ultimately, to a more caring and compassionate society.

Of course, life is never roses all the way. Many mistakes will be made. When new paths are trodden, the way is sometimes uncertain. Some will find it difficult to break the habitual patterns of thought which govern behaviour in a debt-oriented society. No doubt some readers will have already experienced this.

Some will be hard-pressed when the actual exchange value of their investments becomes apparent. Yet, the conversion process can be controlled. Collapse cannot. We should be able, as part of the conversion process, to identify those who might suffer unduly. Then we can be prepared to assist them and cushion any hardship.

The case for honest money is a compelling one. Honest money is not a thief. It does not steal from the thrifty. It is not socially divisive. It does not promote economic and business cycles, creating unemployment. On the contrary, it encourages thrift. It promotes sustainable economic growth. It rewards merit. It demands integrity.

These are worthwhile goals. They can be achieved. What is needed now is the will to make them happen.

John Tomlinson, a Canadian, is an Oxford based economist. He studied business administration at Florida State University in America and practised as a stockbroker with Thomson & McKinnon, a member of the New York Stock Exchange, before he married an English girl and came to live in the United Kingdom.

Having studied the effect of debt on the economies of developed and less developed countries, he set up and is Chairman of Oxford Research and Development Corporation Limited which explores the use of equity instruments and the development of equity markets for areas of finance currently served by debt.

At the invitation of Government Ministers, John Tomlinson is currently investigating the potential for private sector investment in affordable housing.